First published in Great Britain in 2026 by Mitchell Beazley, an imprint of
Octopus Publishing Group Ltd
Carmelite House
50 Victoria Embankment
London EC4Y 0DZ
www.octopusbooks.co.uk

An Hachette UK Company
www.hachette.co.uk

The authorized representative in the EEA is Hachette Ireland,
8 Castlecourt Centre, Dublin 15, D15 XTP3, Ireland (email: info@hbgi.ie)

Originally published as *Cavoli & Merende* in Italy by EDT srl, 17 via Pianezza, 10149 Torino, Italy



Distributed in the US by Hachette Book Group
1290 Avenue of the Americas, 4th and 5th Floors
New York, NY 10104

Distributed in Canada by Canadian Manda Group
664 Annette St., Toronto, Ontario, Canada M6S 2C8



ISBN: 978-1-84601-728-5
eISBN: 978-1-84601-743-8

A CIP catalogue record for this book is available from the British Library.

Printed and bound in China.

10 9 8 7 6 5 4 3 2 1

**English edition 2026**
Commissioning editor Jeannie Stanley
Creative director Jonathan Christie
Designer Jeremy Tilston
Senior editor Alex Stetter
Translated by Luca Calvani
Translation revised by Alexandra Fletcher
Assistant production manager Allison Gonsalves

**Italian edition 2024**
Photography Edoardo Colombo
Illustrations Andrea Tarella
Food stylist Benedetta Canala
Styling Alessandro Franchini
Editor Luca Iaccarino
Editorial manager Isabella Maria
Editorial staff Carlotta Fresi
Design and layout Noemi Roasio and Paolo Racca, Bosio.Associati

# A TUSCAN TABLE

## SEASONAL VEGETARIAN RECIPES FROM ITALY

*With illustrations by*
ANDREA TARELLA

*And photographs by*
EDOARDO COLOMBO

LUCA CALVANI

MITCHELL BEAZLEY

# CONTENTS

*Le Gusciane, Pontemazzori, 15 October 2023*

*It's 5:55am. The farmhouse kitchen is still in shadow, dawn is about to break, but night has not yet quite surrendered to morning. The small lamp on the kitchen counter is the only light revealing the shapes in the room. I love this little lamp – it always stays on, like the light that is always kept lit on a stage at night, to guide the ghosts that roam the theatre.*

*I like to think about how transient all this is; how I've taken up the baton of caring for this house. Though I feel it is entirely mine, I am, in truth, only a temporary custodian.*

*The beep of the local bus echoes in the distance. It comes from Lucca, and after travelling along the Freddana road, it's rounding the first hairpin bend on the descent from Montemagno. From there, you can see the whole Camaiore valley: the imposing Matanna and Prana mountains, their pastures striped with rock, and Mount Gabberi with its deep green forests that turn blue at sunset.*

*The rustling of the tall pine in front of the house reminds me that autumn is here. Even though the leaves on the sweet gum trees in the garden haven't yet changed colour, the highest tips are beginning to blush red. It won't be long now.*

*There's the bus again, this time the horn barely audible; it must have reached the hairpin bend on the opposite slope, towards Nocchi. The concave shape of the valley creates an echo, so it sounds less like the beep of a bus and more like the foghorn of an old steamboat. Now the bus has just one curve left, the last on the Montemagno road, before it arrives in the valley and vanishes from sight.*

*I've always been very fond of that road, the zigzag of tall lime trees unrolling down a hillside of olive groves. And there's the last beep: the bus will stop in a few moments at the Nocchi-Pontemazzori stop and, if it's on time, that means it's 7:08 and I need to get to the market before the best vegetables are gone.*

Le Gusciane

# LIFE, LOVE AND COOKING

In life, we often find ourselves making choices that change the course of our existence. Some may be bold, courageous and a little bumpy. Others can lead to new horizons, surprising discoveries and a deep sense of fulfilment. Moving to live in this farmhouse was one of those choices.

My passion for cooking began on the other side of the ocean, when, still very young, I left Italy to settle in New York. The longing for home and the flavours of Tuscany was strong. I needed to recreate those tastes, surround myself with those aromas, comfort myself a little in that big city, far from the security of friends and family in Prato. But it was there, in that bustling metropolis, that I discovered the magic, sharing and conviviality that Italian cooking can create.

By day I worked in an office in the Garment District; in the evening I was a waiter. I needed to be among people, to ease the loneliness of being in a faraway city. In the warm kitchen of Tanti Baci – a small Italian restaurant in Greenwich Village – I found a refuge. The scent of garlic and basil brought me back home, while the sound of laughter and conversation made me feel part of a big family. It was the family of Paula Toppani, an Italo-Argentine who made us pray to Saint Anthony every evening before starting the dinner service.

Food became my bridge between two worlds; a universal language capable of crossing all cultural or linguistic barriers. The shyness of a young Italian in such a vast and frenetic city melted away in front of a plate of spaghetti al pomodoro; a shared margherita pizza; a table laid with antipasti and wine.

Since then, I have felt at home in every kitchen I've found myself in. The heat under the pans, the fragrance of flavours blending in the air, plates and cutlery moving in a harmonious dance... For me, all this is a form of communication, a way to tell my story, to care for the people I love, to introduce myself to strangers. And the wonder of it! Even now, after thirty years, every time I succeed in creating a delicious dish, I feel something beyond satisfaction. Last March, I made ribollita for the first time at my home, Le Gusciane. I finally managed to summon the exact, intense aroma that took me back to my grandmother Dina's kitchen after nearly three decades. It was perfect. My husband Alessandro looked at me, puzzled at my overwhelming happiness. To him, it was just a soup; to me, it meant much more: I had created a direct link to my childhood and my beloved grandmother.

Scents and flavours have the power to fix memories, to evoke emotions. Every dish tells a story, every ingredient is a character, and every page of a recipe is a journey. The journey of this book begins in the hills of Camaiore, among the olive trees that surround our farm, but extends far beyond, embracing the encounters and places of a lifetime, the little treasures I've gathered on my wanderings across the world. This is not just a collection of recipes; it is a diary, a window into a life full of authentic flavours and extraordinary adventures.

From the crowded streets of New York to the tranquillity of the Camaiore hills, every experience has contributed to the creation of Le Gusciane. This place is not only a retreat for the soul, but the stage on which I continue to tell my stories.

I like to think that, at Le Gusciane, every sensory aspect is cared for, from the background music playing in the shared spaces to the scent of clary sage in the toiletries our guests find in their rooms. We serve our own aromatic helichrysum gin, the bed linens are made exclusively for us and the lighting is carefully designed to create a feeling of warmth and intimacy. To me, it became obvious that I needed to devote myself to the food we serve as well: I couldn't leave that to chance, or in the hands of a hired cook. I had to turn my hobby into something more, to challenge myself and see if I was able to cook consistently at a high level, creating a style worthy of the farmhouse. That's when I realized that Le Gusciane was becoming something vital to me, a place where I could unleash my creativity in a way that working in film or TV would never allow. I could tell stories, create a whole world and – like a set designer, a director of photography and a director – shape it all with fragrances, colours, fabrics and flavours.

In these pages, I would like to take you on a journey not only through recipes, but also through the very fabric of our lives at Le Gusciane, following the rhythm of the seasons – from the warm embrace of summer to the magical atmosphere of winter. I will introduce you to our dachshunds and describe our relationship with the animals that live on the farm. I will speak of the gratitude we feel for the bees buzzing in our garden and for the trees growing quietly around us. I will reveal how the rooms and furnishings of our refuge were conceived, a corner of pure Tuscan lifestyle. Hospitality and food are the way we tell stories of sharing and love. I hope every page will bring you closer to the beauty of conviviality and the magic of real food.

*Welcome to Le Gusciane.*
*Welcome to my story.*

# ESSENTIALS

*Pasta, focaccia, vegetables and sauces for all seasons.*

# CECINA

*A Tuscan flatbread made with chickpea (garbanzo bean) flour and known elsewhere in Italy as farinata, cecina holds a special place in my heart because it was one of my father's favourite foods. Every year on our way back from the beach at the end of the summer, the car loaded with all our holiday luggage, we would stop at a pizzeria on the seafront in Viareggio. There, with the sea breeze in the air and the sunset colouring the horizon, we would savour the delicious thin and crispy cecina. I love making these when my sister Eva comes over for dinner, because I know that, beyond enjoying the taste, she shares those family memories with me.*

INGREDIENTS
*Serves 4*

- 180g (1½ cups) gram (chickpea/garbanzo bean) flour
- 600ml (2½ cups) water
- 2 tablespoons extra virgin olive oil, plus extra for the tin
- 1½ teaspoons salt
- rosemary leaves
- freshly ground black pepper

In a bowl, combine the gram flour with the water using a hand blender. Skim off any foam with a spoon, cover with a tea towel and leave to rest for a couple of hours.

After the resting time, preheat the oven to 220°C (425°F), Gas Mark 7. Oil a baking tin well; my favourite tin for this bread is about 36cm (14¼ inches) in diameter, but if you don't have one like that, find an equivalent that means the batter will lie only about 5–6mm (¼ inch) deep. Place the oiled tin in the oven – it's important that it is very hot when you pour in the batter, to help the base of the cecina to become beautifully crisp.

Add the olive oil and salt to the batter, stirring well to dissolve any flour that may have settled at the bottom of the bowl.

Carefully open the oven and slowly pour the batter into the hot tin, taking care not to burn yourself. Close the oven and bake for 45–50 minutes. Depending on the flour, cooking times may vary; the cecina is ready when you no longer see the wobble of bubbles beneath the surface. Remove from the oven, leave to cool for 5 minutes, then finish with a sprinkling of rosemary leaves and freshly ground black pepper.

# THREE FLAVOURS OF FOCACCIA

*My mother had a passion for focaccia, which in Tuscany we call schiacciata. She would buy it warm from the bakery before picking us up from school and place it between the front seats of the car, and as soon as we climbed in, we'd rush to grab a piece. Even when we were at the beach, in Forte dei Marmi, we loved buying small focaccias in the town square. In short, focaccia has always been in our family's DNA. This was one of the recipes that took me the longest to master, but when I finally did, the satisfaction was immense. Smelling the aroma of focaccia wafting through the farmhouse is, for me, both a true celebration and a way to remember my mother.*

INGREDIENTS
*Makes 3*

*For the dough*

- 25g (1oz) fresh yeast, or 7g (¼oz) fast-action dried yeast
- 2 teaspoons sugar
- 300ml (1¼ cups) warm water
- 500g (4 cups) plain flour
- 2 teaspoons salt
- 2 teaspoons barley malt (optional)
- 1½ tablespoons extra virgin olive oil, plus extra for oiling, frying and topping

*For courgette focaccia*

- 2 courgettes (zucchini)
- 1 unpeeled garlic clove

*For caramelized onion focaccia*

- 2 large red onions
- extra virgin olive oil
- 2 tablespoons brown sugar
- 1 tablespoon balsamic vinegar
- rosemary leaves, to serve (optional)

*For tomato and olive focaccia*

- 10 cherry tomatoes
- 100g (½ cup) olives (ideally Tuscan, such as Barese)
- sea salt flakes
- dried or fresh oregano

Dissolve the yeast and sugar in 100ml (about ½ cup) of the warm water. Leave for 10 minutes, until a foam forms.

In a large bowl, combine the flour with the salt. Add the activated yeast, the malt, if using, and the remaining warm water. Knead, drizzling in the olive oil, until you have a smooth and elastic dough. Cover and leave to rest for 1 hour.

Next, perform a fold: roll the dough into a rectangle, fold one third towards the centre, then fold the other third over it; rotate the dough 90 degrees and repeat the fold. Do this once an hour for a total of 3 times. After the last fold, shape the dough into a ball and place it in an oiled bowl. Cover with clingfilm and leave to rise in a warm place for 2 hours, or until doubled in size.

Oil three round cake tins; mine measure 18cm (7 inches) at their base and 20cm (8 inches) at the rim. Divide the dough into 3 equal pieces and stretch each into a tin, dimpling the surface with your fingertips.

For the courgette focaccia, slice the courgettes into thin rounds and sauté them in a pan with a drizzle of olive oil and the unpeeled garlic clove. Spread over the dough surface.

For the caramelized onion focaccia, slice the onions and cook them in a pan with a drizzle of olive oil, the brown sugar and balsamic vinegar. Simmer until the onions are soft and caramelized. Spread over the dough surface.

For the tomato and olive focaccia, halve the cherry tomatoes and distribute them with the olives over the dough. Sprinkle with salt, oregano and a drizzle of olive oil.

In each case, after adding the toppings, cover and leave for another 30 minutes.

Preheat the oven to 220°C (425°F), Gas Mark 7 and bake the focaccias for 20–25 minutes, or until golden and crisp. Scatter the onion focaccia with rosemary leaves, if you like, to serve.

# CHRISTIAN'S MULTIGRAIN FOCACCIA

*For any cooking enthusiast, finding mentors who welcome and nurture your passion is essential. In my case, Debora, Katia, Emanuel and Christian – the siblings behind Pasticceria Rossano – stand out. Not only do they make the best croissants in Camaiore, they've also become my trusted bread-baking advisors. Their wholegrain focaccia, in particular, is an example of how the simplest ingredients can be elevated into something truly delicious.*

*When you want a superior-quality focaccia, incorporating a biga into the dough is essential. This pre-ferment not only enriches the bread's flavour and aroma but also improves its digestibility, thanks to the long fermentation. If you're short on time or prefer a more straightforward approach, you can work with the second dough alone, but perform three folding cycles (see page 17) to improve the bread's structure.*

**INGREDIENTS**
*Serves 4*

*For the biga (starter dough)*

- 10g (¼oz) fresh yeast, or 3g (½ teaspoon) fast-action dried yeast
- 350g (1½ cups) water
- 700g (5½ cups) multigrain flour with seeds

*For the second dough*

- 5g (⅛oz) fresh yeast, or 2g (½ teaspoon) fast-action dried yeast
- 1 tablespoon barley malt
- 400g (1¾ cups) water
- 300g (2½ cups) multigrain flour with seeds
- 1 tablespoon salt
- 1 tablespoon extra virgin olive oil
- sea salt flakes

For the biga, place the yeast in a large bowl and dissolve it completely in the water to ensure even fermentation. Gradually add the flour, stirring well to avoid lumps. The goal is a smooth, homogeneous dough. Let it rest at room temperature for 1 hour, then refrigerate for 18 hours. This step is crucial to develop the ideal aroma and texture.

For the second dough, start by dissolving the yeast and malt in a large bowl containing the water – this helps activate the yeast more effectively. Gradually add the flour, continuing to stir for a smooth consistency. Add the salt only after most of the flour has been absorbed so as not to hinder the yeast's activity.

Knead vigorously until the dough is smooth and elastic, then incorporate the olive oil and knead until fully absorbed. Let the dough rise in a warm place until doubled in volume; 1–2 hours.

Transfer the dough to a rectangular baking tin – mine measures 35 × 28cm (14 × 11 inches) – dimple the focaccia with your fingers and let it rest for another 20–30 minutes.

Preheat the oven to 220°C (425°F), Gas Mark 7, scatter the focaccia with sea salt flakes and bake for 20–25 minutes.

# ROASTED VEGETABLES

*As a child, I was never a fan of vegetables, but my sister Eva adored them, whether they were raw, boiled or roasted. When my mother made peperonata (pepper stew), the aroma would fill the house, so when dinner time came, Eva would sit at the table, beaming, a piece of bread already in her hand to wipe the plate clean. Over the years, my aversion to vegetables turned into devotion, and I owe this change to dishes like this one. Today, every time I chop vegetables to make it, I can't help but think back to those days. And I smile, recognizing how much our tastes evolve over a lifetime.*

**INGREDIENTS**
*Serves 4*

- 1 sweet potato
- 1 beetroot (beet)
- 1 Jerusalem artichoke
- ½ cauliflower
- 1 head of regular broccoli
- 1 head of Romanesco broccoli
- 4 unpeeled garlic cloves
- 3–4 tablespoons extra virgin olive oil
- 2 teaspoons thyme leaves
- salt and freshly ground black pepper

Preheat the oven to 200°C (400°F), Gas Mark 6.

Peel the sweet potato, beetroot and Jerusalem artichoke, then cut into 2cm (¾ inch) cubes. Break the cauliflower and both types of broccoli into small florets.

In a large bowl, combine all the vegetables, the garlic cloves, olive oil, thyme, salt and pepper. Toss well to ensure everything is well coated.

Spread the vegetables evenly over 1–2 baking sheets lined with baking paper. Make sure they lie in a single layer for even roasting.

Bake for 25–30 minutes, or until the vegetables are golden and tender. Toss once halfway through cooking to ensure they are evenly browned.

# VARENA'S POMAROLA WITH SPAGHETTI

*Varena is a straightforward woman with a unique approach to Tuscan cooking. Many traditional regional recipes are rich and robust, but Varena tends to make them more delicate. A perfect example of her style is this pomarola. Unlike classic versions, Varena's is made without a soffritto base of onion, carrot and celery. The result is a light yet flavourful sauce that enhances the pure taste of the tomatoes. Her cooking reflects her personality: simple, direct and authentic.*

**INGREDIENTS**
*Serves 4*

- 1kg (2lb 4oz) tomatoes, preferably San Marzano or plum
- extra virgin olive oil
- handful of basil
- 320g (11½oz) spaghetti
- knob of butter
- grated Parmesan cheese (optional)
- salt

Wash the tomatoes, place them in a small saucepan and add just enough water to cover them. Bring to the boil and blanch until the skins start to wrinkle and peel away easily; 5–10 minutes.

Remove the tomatoes from the water and let them cool slightly. Pass them through a food mill to obtain a smooth sauce, discarding the skins and seeds.

Pour the tomato sauce into a saucepan. Add a generous drizzle of olive oil and a good pinch of salt, then simmer gently for 20–30 minutes, stirring occasionally. Towards the end of cooking, tear in most of the basil leaves.

Cook the spaghetti in plenty of salted boiling water according to the packet instructions. Drain when al dente, reserving a little of the cooking water.

In a large frying pan, melt the knob of butter. Add the drained spaghetti and a ladleful of the reserved cooking water. Add the pomarola and toss well over a medium heat.

Add the grated Parmesan, if using, and continue tossing until you achieve a creamy consistency. Serve the spaghetti hot, scattered with the remaining basil leaves and a drizzle of olive oil.

# POTATO SKINS

*Whenever I cook potatoes, I scrub them first, then peel them, putting the peels to soak in water. If necessary, I even refrigerate the peelings for a day because the more water they absorb, the crispier and tastier they become when roasted. I learned this trick in the United States, where potato skins are often served as snacks with drinks. Here in Italy, our guests are often surprised when we serve them potato skins. It is definitely a fun idea, and you can get creative with the toppings. You could add chopped rosemary, thyme or oregano leaves before roasting, or experiment with sweet or smoked paprika, curry powder or chilli powder. For a richer flavour, sprinkle the skins with grated Parmesan or Cheddar cheese during the last 5 minutes of roasting. Garlic lovers can add garlic powder or finely minced garlic before roasting. For a tangy touch, drizzle a little balsamic vinegar over the skins just after they come out of the oven.*

**INGREDIENTS**
*Serves 4*

- potatoes, as many as desired
- extra virgin olive oil
- salt and freshly ground black pepper

Scrub the potatoes thoroughly to remove any traces of soil. Peel them, discarding any damaged or blemished pieces. Place the peelings in a bowl of cold water and let them soak for about 10 minutes (or even overnight in the refrigerator – see above). This helps remove excess starch and makes them crispier.

Preheat the oven to 200°C (400°F), Gas Mark 6.

Drain the potato peelings well and pat them dry with a tea towel or kitchen paper. Arrange them on a baking sheet lined with baking paper. Using a pastry brush, coat them evenly with olive oil and add a generous twist of black pepper.

Bake for 20–25 minutes, or until golden and crispy, tossing halfway through to ensure even browning. Once ready, season with salt and serve hot.

# VEGETARIAN RAGÙ FOR MARCO

*Ragù is a serious matter. When I was a child, there was the ragù my maternal grandmother made, which my mother often made too, sometimes with a few variations of her own, and then there was my paternal grandmother's ragù, which I particularly loved. Instead of minced beef, Nonna Ottavia used thin slices of meat, cooked and shredded, to avoid her sauce having a grainy texture. The meat-free version below is truly delicious and perfect for my brother Marco, who lives in California and often cooks for vegetarians. To recreate the texture of a classic bolognese sauce, I use lentils and cashews. Every time this sauce meets a scattering of Parmesan, it takes me right back to my childhood.*

**INGREDIENTS**
*Serves 4*

- 200g (1 cup) brown or green lentils
- 1 litre (4 cups) vegetable stock (broth)
- 1 onion
- 3 celery sticks
- 3 carrots
- extra virgin olive oil
- 1 bay leaf, chopped
- 120g (scant 1 cup) chopped cashew nuts
- 240ml (1 cup) dry white wine
- 240ml (1 cup) tomato passata
- salt
- oregano leaves, to serve (optional)

Rinse the lentils, then soak for about 6 hours in cold water. Drain and rinse well.

Pour the stock into a saucepan, place over a medium heat and add the drained lentils. Season with salt and cook for about 30 minutes.

Finely dice the onion and celery and grate the carrots, or just chop them all together in a food processor. Sauté the vegetables in oil in a saucepan until the onion is translucent. Add the chopped bay leaf and season with salt.

Add the chopped cashews and the drained lentils. As soon as the mixture returns to the boil, pour in the white wine, cover and reduce the heat.

Cook for about 20 minutes, then add the passata. Simmer over a low heat for 45 minutes, stirring occasionally and adjusting the seasoning, as well as adding a drizzle of olive oil to prevent the lentils from breaking down too much. Scatter with oregano leaves, if you like, to serve.

# VEGAN RICOTTA

*This is a discovery I made on a recent trip to Los Angeles. My friend Tamara, who works as both a music producer and a life coach, has followed a plant-based diet for more than a decade. One of the things that surprised me the most was the variety of cheeses she made at home, using different kinds of nuts. This very quick recipe for vegan ricotta was one of them. Enjoy it on toast, or use to enrich vegetable soups, or drizzle with olive oil and use it as a dip for crudités.*

**INGREDIENTS**
*Serves 4*

- 200g (1½ cups) cashew nuts
- juice of 1 lemon
- salt

Soak the cashews in water for a couple of hours. Drain and rinse them, then blend with the lemon juice, adding a little water to help emulsify the mixture. Season with salt to taste.

# FRESH EGG PASTA DOUGH

*Ever since childhood, I have regarded the making of fresh pasta dough with a mixture of admiration and apprehension. It was the realm of grandmothers, whose expert hands could transform simple ingredients into works of art. For years, I was convinced that making fresh pasta was too complex for me. However, as I grew older, I discovered that once you master the technique, it becomes a pleasant creative ritual, far less intimidating than I once imagined.*

**INGREDIENTS**
*Serves 4*

- 850g (7⅓ cups) '00' flour
- 150g (1 scant cup) semolina
- 5 eggs
- 1 tablespoon extra virgin olive oil
- 150ml (⅔ cup) whole milk
- salt

Place the flour and semolina on a work surface, reserving a handful to use later for rolling, and form a well in the centre. Crack the eggs into the well, then add the olive oil, milk and a generous pinch of salt.

Work quickly with your fingertips until you have a firm ball of dough. If you have a stand mixer, this process will be quicker, but I still recommend finishing with a few kneads by hand. Once you have a smooth and consistent ball of dough, wrap it in a tea towel and let it rest in the refrigerator for about 1 hour.

After resting, cut the dough into wedges with a pastry cutter. Roll out each piece with the help of some flour. I use a pasta machine, and a trick I have learned to achieve a rustic texture is to pass the strips through once at the widest setting, dust them with flour, let them rest for 10 minutes, then roll them through again, this time on the thinnest setting. This gives the pasta a rough surface that makes it more porous, allowing it to absorb sauces better.

# TRIO OF PESTOS

*Pesto is a quick and versatile sauce, and, for me, it was a late discovery: I was 19 years old and in Florence, at a friend's house. It was love at first taste. Over the years, I discovered other truly exceptional versions, such as the celery pesto below which I learned from chef Giulio at Candalla, a beautiful restaurant in Camaiore. Another comes from my friend Lisa, who preserves vegetables in her factory in Tuscany; her sun-dried tomatoes make a truly unique pesto. Each of these three pestos has a story behind it, a connection with special people and places.*

**INGREDIENTS**
*Serves 4*

*For the Classic Pesto*

- 50g (2½ cups loosely packed) basil leaves
- 30g (¼ cup) pine nuts
- 50g (½ cup) grated pecorino cheese
- 50g (½ cup) grated Parmesan cheese
- 100ml extra virgin olive oil
- salt

*For the Celery, Pistachio and Lime Pesto*

- 30g (1½ cups loosely packed) celery leaves
- 50g (⅓ cup) shelled unsalted pistachios
- 50g (½ cup) grated Parmesan cheese
- finely grated zest and juice of 1 lime
- 100ml (½ cup) extra virgin olive oil

*For the Sun-Dried Tomato and Almond Pesto*

- 100g (⅔ cup) sun-dried tomatoes in oil
- 50g (½ cup) blanched almonds
- 50g (½ cup) grated Parmesan cheese
- basil leaves (optional)
- 100ml (½ cup) extra virgin olive oil

To make the classic pesto, wash and dry the basil. In a mortar or blender, crush the pine nuts with a pinch of salt. Add the basil leaves a little at a time, crushing them gently to avoid oxidation (blackening). Incorporate the pecorino and Parmesan, stirring well. Slowly pour in the olive oil, continuing to stir until you reach a creamy consistency. Adjust the salt if needed.

For the celery pesto, wash the celery leaves. In a blender, combine the leaves and pistachios and blend until you have a smooth paste. Add the Parmesan, lime zest and juice, stirring well. Slowly pour in the olive oil, blending until creamy. Adjust the salt if needed.

To make the sun-dried tomato pesto, drain the tomatoes of excess oil. In a blender, combine the tomatoes and almonds and blend until smooth. Add the Parmesan and, if desired, a few basil leaves. Slowly pour in the olive oil, blending until creamy. Adjust the salt if needed.

# AUTUMN

*The leaves change colour, the air turns crisp, the crickets fall silent and the pace of life slows. At this time of year, my kitchen is filled with recipes for comfort.*

I believe my love for autumn was born in New York City. Growing up in Prato, where September meant merely the arrival of rain, I had never fully experienced autumn's magic. There were, of course, those October Sundays when my father would take us to the woods of Schignano or Bacchereto to gather chestnuts; I treasure those memories. Yet the true spark, the moment I fell for autumn, only came a few years later, after crossing the ocean.

When I first moved to New York in 1994, I looked forward to the weekends as a chance to wander the city's neighbourhoods. So that October, only a few months after arriving in the United States, I was surprised when my American girlfriend Jacqueline, who had moved to New York from Los Angeles, announced that the following weekend we would be driving to Connecticut 'to see the leaves'. At the time, I had no idea how much 'fall' was celebrated in the United States. On the East Coast, the changing colours of autumn are not only admired but *studied*. At the weekends, television weather reports track the movement of the foliage colour belt as it shifts from north to south, pinpointing where and when you can witness the phenomenon at its peak.

*October advances, and with it come the first cool winds from the North. Suddenly, the crickets fall silent, and the streets of Camaiore seem quieter, emptier, after the summer visitors have gone.*

Intrigued, I got in the car and we left Manhattan behind, heading north. Nothing could have prepared me for what I was about to see. Standing on a lookout point, I found myself speechless before an endless expanse of rolling hills ablaze with every shade from crimson to gold to fiery orange.

It was on that day that I fell in love with American sweet gum trees, aka liquidambars. We later planted them in our Tuscan garden, and they are now turning red outside our farmhouse as October paints its colours on the landscape once more. Certain moments stay with us forever, like that afternoon in Connecticut, which has left a trace here, at our home in Italy.

Life at the farmhouse slows down as well. Our days take on a gentler rhythm, giving us time to notice, day by day, the subtle changes of the season. Alessandro starts stacking wood in the oak and chestnut grove behind the house; with the end of the honeydew-collecting season, the bees quieten down and you can walk near the hives without having to wear a veil. The carpet of fallen leaves deepens; soon it will be as thick as a mattress. The more fragile chestnut leaves, in shades of orange and brown, mingle with those of the alders and oaks, tinged with pale pink, while on the lawn the sweet gum trees put on the most spectacular show. Their leaves shift gradually from green to vermilion, creating the effect of broad brushstrokes of paint across the foliage and making a striking contrast with the green grass at their feet.

By November, the farmhouse stoves are lit. Our little sitting room becomes my refuge, the place where I settle in to work by the warmth of the fire. The tapping of the keyboard blends with the crackle of the wood in the stove. The dachshunds doze in their basket and sometimes I see them twitch in their sleep, chasing deer through a forest of dreams.

During this season, being in the kitchen feels more like a pleasure than a duty. The abundance of pumpkins and cavolo nero rekindles my creativity, urging me to experiment with Tuscan autumn soups, such as incavolata or minestra sulla palla. Then comes the arrival of the new olive oil, fiery and sharp with a note of artichoke, a delight best savoured with the unsalted Tuscan bread: panaccio.

Evenings with friends are frequent; we gather, ten of us around the table, to knead pizza dough and prepare panzerotti filled with stracchino cheese, before ending the night with a game of Scrabble. Yet what linger most vividly in my memory are the solitary moments of contemplation, such as returning from a walk in the woods at sunset, when the sky deepens into pink and violet, and the red canopies of Mount Gabberi and Mount Matanna are set ablaze.

Autumn at the farmhouse is a season of change and enchantment, inviting us to slow down and savour the small joys of life, to rediscover the warmth and beauty of tradition.

# EGGS FLORENTINE

*When I was in New York as a young drama student, I had very specific ideas about how I would spend my days as a film star, which played in my mind almost like comic strips. One of those scenes saw me spending mornings studying scripts at a table at Balthazar, an elegant French-style brasserie on Spring Street. The place was famous for its small bakery, where they made baguettes and a naturally leavened bread with a dark, crunchy crust: the perfect companion for eggs. Every time I make eggs Florentine, I am transported back there, among the waiters arranging seafood platters on shimmering mountains of ice in the mirrored dining room to a soundtrack of classical music.*

**INGREDIENTS**
*Serves 4*

- 500g (1lb 2oz) spinach
- extra virgin olive oil
- 1 garlic clove, lightly crushed
- pinch of chilli flakes, plus extra to serve
- 1 tablespoon white wine vinegar
- 4 eggs
- 4 slices of multigrain or rustic Italian bread
- salt

Wash the spinach, removing the stems and tougher ribs, then blanch in boiling water for 1½ minutes. Drain and transfer to a wide pan with a drizzle of olive oil and the crushed garlic clove. Sauté briefly to let the spinach absorb the flavour, adding the chilli flakes and a little salt.

Meanwhile, bring a small saucepan of water to the boil, with the vinegar and a pinch of salt. Crack one egg at a time into a small sieve to remove the thinner part of the white. Reduce the heat under the saucepan, swirl the water to create a vortex, and gently drop in the egg. Poach for about 2 minutes, until the white is set but the yolk is still soft. Remove with a slotted spoon and repeat with the remaining eggs.

Toast the bread, keeping the inside of the slices tender. Brush or drizzle with olive oil, sprinkle with salt while still warm, then top with a layer of spinach. Finish each slice with a poached egg, another drizzle of oil, a little more salt and a dusting of chilli flakes.

# CRISPY EGG WITH BUTTERNUT SQUASH VELOUTÉ AND KALE CHIPS

*During the years I spent as a judge on* Cortesie per gli Ospiti *– an Italian TV show about hospitality and home entertaining – I was on a panel with two wonderful colleagues: Csaba dalla Zorza, who oversaw lifestyle, and Roberto Valbuzzi, a professional chef in charge of the food. I was the judge for interior design, evaluating the style and atmosphere of the hosts' homes. Long days on set were filled with lively conversations, and in our downtime, we often exchanged recipes. This one came from Roberto. Although it requires a little technique, the dish is otherwise simple to prepare and it always makes a stunning impression.*

### INGREDIENTS
*Serves 4*

- 1 small bunch of cavolo nero, about 150g (5½oz)
- extra virgin olive oil
- 1 small butternut squash, about 700–800g (1lb 9oz–1lb 12oz)
- 50g (3½ tablespoons) unsalted butter
- 1 tablespoon white wine vinegar
- 5 eggs
- groundnut or sunflower oil
- 100g (1 cup) breadcrumbs
- salt and freshly ground black pepper

Preheat the oven to 180°C (350°F), Gas Mark 4.

Wash and prepare the cavolo nero, removing the tough stems, then spread the leaves out on a baking sheet lined with greaseproof paper. Drizzle with olive oil and sprinkle lightly with salt. Clean the butternut squash, then cut it in half, remove the seeds, brush with olive oil and season with salt. Place the squash halves in a baking tray.

Place both trays in the oven. Remove the cavolo nero after about 10 minutes, or once dry and crisp, then set aside. Continue baking the squash for another 40 minutes or so, until tender. Scoop out the cooked flesh, blend with the butter and adjust the seasoning to make a smooth velouté.

Bring a small saucepan of water to the boil, with the vinegar and a pinch of salt. Crack one egg at a time into a small sieve to remove the thinner part of the white. Reduce the heat under the saucepan, swirl the water to create a vortex, and gently drop in the egg. Poach until the white is set but the yolk is still soft. Remove with a slotted spoon to a bowl of cold water and repeat with 3 more eggs (reserve the fifth).

Heat the groundnut or sunflower oil in a small pan. Beat the remaining egg in a bowl and place the breadcrumbs in a wide, shallow dish. Dip each poached egg in the beaten egg, then roll gently in the breadcrumbs. Deep-fry for about 1 minute, until golden and crisp, then remove with a slotted spoon.

To serve, spoon some of the butternut squash velouté onto each plate, making neat quenelles if you like. Place the crispy egg in the centre and scatter crumbled cavolo nero chips on top. Finish with a twist of black pepper.

# CELERIAC AND APPLE CARPACCIO

*Encounters with others enrich every place and each experience. Meeting Roberta certainly made my stay at a beautiful wellness centre in Castrocaro much more enjoyable. Between treatments and check-ups, we would often run into each other in the hallways. At the table, considering the meagre calories of the meals being served, we dreamed together of lasagne and towering ice cream sundaes. One day, however, the chef wowed us with this recipe, which I tried to recreate as soon as I got home. Celeriac is rather underrated, but its fragrance and texture make it perfect for a light, refreshing carpaccio.*

**INGREDIENTS**
*Serves 4*

- 1 head of celeriac
- 2 Golden Delicious apples
- 1 fresh turmeric root
- 2 tablespoons apple cider vinegar
- 4 tablespoons extra virgin olive oil, or to taste
- 30g (¼ cup) finely chopped pistachios
- freshly ground black pepper

Peel the celeriac with a vegetable peeler. Wash the apples and remove the cores and seeds, ideally with an apple corer, if you have one.

Take a large serving tray and set a mandoline to its thinnest setting. Slice the celeriac directly on to the tray, letting the slices fall naturally so they curl slightly and resemble large tulip petals. Do the same with the apples, layering them so that the apple and celeriac 'petals' overlap in a casual pattern.

For the dressing, peel the turmeric root and dice it. Place the pieces in a blender or hand-blend with the vinegar until smooth. Then whisk in the olive oil. Typically, vinaigrette should have twice as much oil as vinegar, but you can adjust that depending on the acidity of your vinegar and to your taste.

Drizzle the carpaccio with the dressing, then finish with a scattering of chopped pistachios and a twist of black pepper.

STAUB

# MEDITERRANEAN SALAD WITH SQUASH, COURGETTE AND FETA

*I met Kevin at an event in New York. He ran a communications agency that worked with a major Italian fashion group, and when we were introduced, he immediately launched into his repertoire of Italian. He was hilarious, brilliant and full of energy, and that evening marked the beginning of our friendship. In the years that followed, whenever he passed through London, we would always meet for dinner in Notting Hill. One evening, in a small Mediterranean restaurant, we ate a dish with squash and feta. I tried to recreate it at home, and, after several attempts, I think I have finally succeeded. Perhaps I should ask Kevin what he thinks of the result…*

**INGREDIENTS**
*Serves 4*

*For the salad*

- ½ small butternut squash, peeled and cut into chunks, about 550g (1lb 4oz) prepared weight
- 2½ tablespoons extra virgin olive oil
- 3–4 yellow or green courgettes (zucchini), about 500g (1lb 2oz) total weight
- 1 tablespoon clear honey
- 2 garlic cloves, crushed
- 1 tablespoon apple cider vinegar
- 2 tablespoons roughly chopped tarragon leaves
- 250g (1 cup) ricotta cheese
- 3 tablespoons Greek yogurt
- 100g (3½oz) feta cheese
- finely grated zest and juice of 1 lemon
- salt and freshly ground black pepper

*For the topping*

- 50g (⅓ cup) shelled unsalted pistachios, roughly chopped
- ½ teaspoon coriander seeds, lightly crushed
- ¾ teaspoon chilli flakes
- handful of mint leaves

Preheat the oven to 200°C (400°F), Gas Mark 6.

Place the squash in a large bowl with 1½ tablespoons of the olive oil, ¾ teaspoon of salt and a good twist of black pepper. Toss well, then spread on to a baking sheet lined with baking paper. Roast for 25 minutes, turning halfway through, until tender. Remove from the oven and allow to cool slightly, leaving the oven on.

Meanwhile, warm a griddle pan over a high heat. Cut most of the courgettes into chunks, and finely slice a few lengths into ribbons. Toss the courgette chunks in a large bowl with the remaining 1 tablespoon of olive oil, ½ teaspoon of salt and black pepper. Griddle the courgette chunks, in batches if necessary, for about 3 minutes, turning to get griddle marks on all sides. Transfer to a baking sheet lined with baking paper and roast for 5 minutes, until cooked through but still crisp.

In a large bowl, combine the honey, 1 crushed garlic clove, the apple cider vinegar, tarragon and a pinch of salt. Add the roasted squash and courgettes, tossing gently to coat. Set aside.

In another bowl, mix together the ricotta and Greek yogurt, crumble in 60g (2¼oz) of the feta, then add the lemon zest and juice, the remaining crushed garlic clove and a pinch of salt and black pepper. Whisk until smooth.

Spread the feta cream on to a large serving platter and arrange the courgettes and squash on top, with a few strands of the courgette ribbons you made earlier. Finish by crumbling over the remaining feta, then sprinkle with the pistachios, crushed coriander seeds and chilli flakes. Scatter with mint leaves and serve.

# SAUTÉED ESCAROLE WITH CARAMELIZED ONION, CHESTNUTS AND MISO

*I still remember the first time I tasted escarole – a type of endive – at Pianostrada, a tiny little takeaway tucked into a Trastevere alley. Paola, a banker-turned-chef, has created here in Rome a warm refuge of flavour. She served her escarole with Taggiasca olives, chestnuts, anchovies and burrata on toasted bread. For me, this dish embodied the soul of home cooking, elevated into culinary art. It was among the aromas and flavours of Trastevere, and thanks to the energy of Paola and her daughter, that the dream of dedicating myself to cooking truly took root.*

**INGREDIENTS**
*Serves 4*

- 1 red onion, sliced
- extra virgin olive oil
- 1 tablespoon sugar
- 1 tablespoon apple cider vinegar
- 1 head of escarole
- 40g (¼ cup) raisins
- 2 garlic cloves
- ½ teaspoon chilli flakes
- ½ tablespoon miso paste
- 60g (½ cup) Taggiasca olives
- 10 cooked chestnuts
- 50g (⅓ cup) cashew nuts
- salt and freshly ground black pepper

Begin by preparing the caramelized onion. In a small saucepan, cook the sliced onion with a drizzle of olive oil and a pinch of salt over a low heat, covered, until softened. Increase the heat, add the sugar and deglaze the pan with the apple cider vinegar. After a couple of minutes, reduce the heat, letting the onion caramelize gently.

Wash the escarole and separate the leaves. Soak the raisins in a bowl of hot water.

Warm a wok with olive oil, then peel and crush the garlic cloves, add them to the pan and tilt it so the hot oil covers them. Add the chilli flakes, followed quickly by the escarole leaves. Stir in the miso paste, reduce the heat, cover and let the leaves wilt slowly.

When the stems of the leaves turn translucent, uncover, increase the heat and sauté briefly. Gradually add the drained raisins, the olives, chestnuts and cashews, tossing everything together with tongs or a spoon. Near the end of cooking, add the caramelized onions with another drizzle of olive oil and toss once more.

Serve, with the escarole leaves arranged on the plate and the other ingredients piled on top. Finish with a twist of black pepper and a final drizzle of olive oil.

# CHICKPEA CAKE WITH CASHEW RICOTTA AND GREMOLATA

*I met Kate through Pete, who was my driver while I was shooting a film in London. Kate was also an actor. She had a large apartment in Whitechapel and a spare room – an ideal solution for me. After a year in London, living in a tiny Chelsea flat, I needed something more affordable, and, frankly, I wanted a little company. Living with Kate and her son Ethan turned out to be a perfect fit. The room was beautiful, with a view over the City and of Whitechapel market, which was a real discovery for me. I cherished my evening chats with Kate. She had a surprising ability to endlessly whip up what she called 'improvised dinners', which were always delicious. Thanks to her, I learned to make real use of the oven, which until then I had barely touched.*

**INGREDIENTS**
*Serves 4*

*For the casserole*

- 180g (1½ cups) gram (chickpea/garbanzo bean) flour
- 1 teaspoon salt
- 3 tablespoons extra virgin olive oil
- 1 red onion, sliced
- 30g (1oz) baby spinach
- 2–4 plum tomatoes, diced
- 16 black olives

*For the cashew ricotta*

- 150g (1 cup) cashew nuts
- juice of 1 lemon
- 2 teaspoons extra virgin olive oil
- salt

*For the gremolata*

- handful of parsley leaves
- 1 garlic clove
- juice of 1 lemon
- extra virgin olive oil
- salt

In a jug, combine 600ml (2½ cups) of water with the gram flour and teaspoon of salt. Blend with a hand blender, then let the batter rest, covered with a cloth. Skim off any foam that forms on the surface and blend again with 1 tablespoon of the olive oil.

Soak the cashews in water for 2 hours.

Preheat the oven to 180°C (350°F), Gas Mark 4.

Warm 2 tablespoons of olive oil in a 20cm (8-inch) cast-iron pan over a medium heat. Add the sliced onion and cook for 3 minutes, until softened and lightly golden. Pour in half the batter and add the spinach. Let it cook undisturbed for 2–3 minutes, until the spinach begins to wilt. Add the diced tomatoes and the olives, spreading them evenly over the surface. Pour in the remaining batter, then transfer the pan to the oven and bake for about 20 minutes.

While it is baking, drain the cashews and blend them with the lemon juice, olive oil and a pinch of salt, adding enough water to reach a ricotta-like consistency.

For the gremolata, blend the parsley, garlic, lemon juice, a little olive oil and salt until smooth and vibrant.

Serve the chickpea casserole warm, with both the cashew ricotta and the gremolata on the side.

STAUB
COACHES DAILY

# PUMPKIN GNOCCHI WITH GORGONZOLA CREAM

*After Halloween, pumpkins always abound in our house. Every year we buy an extravagant number of them in nearby Capezzano, but once the celebrations are over, I always find myself looking for creative ways to use them up. One year, my friend Chiara – always on the lookout for new recipes on social media – suggested this brilliant idea. The sweetness of the pumpkin pairs perfectly with the creaminess and strong flavour of Gorgonzola, creating a dish that wins everyone over.*

**INGREDIENTS**
*Serves 4*

*For the kale powder*

- 2–3 cavolo nero leaves
- extra virgin olive oil
- salt

*For the gnocchi*

- 500g (1lb 2oz) pumpkin
- 1 egg
- 50g (½ cup) grated Parmesan cheese
- pinch of nutmeg
- 200g (1½ cups) plain flour, plus extra for dusting
- salt and freshly ground black pepper

*For the cream*

- 30g (2 tablespoons) unsalted butter
- 200ml (¾ cup plus 1 tablespoon) double (heavy) cream
- 200g (7oz) mild Gorgonzola cheese, cut into pieces
- 50g (½ cup) grated Parmesan cheese

Preheat the oven to 180°C (350°F), Gas Mark 4.

While the oven warms, wash the cavolo nero leaves and dry them well. Brush lightly with olive oil, sprinkle with salt and place on a nonstick baking tray. Bake for about 15 minutes, until crisp, let them cool, then grind finely in a mortar to obtain a powder.

Cut the pumpkin into slices, deseed them and place in a baking tray. Roast for 30–40 minutes, until tender. Allow to cool slightly, then remove the skin and mash the flesh with a fork, or pass it through a sieve, to make a smooth purée. Allow to cool.

In a large bowl, combine the cooled pumpkin purée with the egg, grated Parmesan, a dusting of nutmeg and a pinch of salt and pepper. Gradually add the flour until you have a soft, slightly sticky dough, adding more if needed. On a floured surface, roll portions of dough into logs 1–2cm (½–¾ inch) in diameter, then cut into 2cm (¾-inch) pieces. Roll each gnocco over the back of a fork to create ridges.

Bring a large pan of salted water to a boil. Cook the gnocchi in small batches until they float to the surface, then lift them out with a slotted spoon. Transfer to a plate and keep warm.

Meanwhile, prepare the Gorgonzola cream. Melt the butter in a wide frying pan over a medium heat, add the cream and bring to a gentle simmer. Add the Gorgonzola and stir until completely melted. Stir in the Parmesan until the sauce is smooth, seasoning with black pepper to taste.

Toss the freshly drained gnocchi gently in the Gorgonzola cream to coat. Serve hot, with a dusting of the cavolo nero powder and a twist of black pepper.

# MALTAGLIATI WITH CONFIT TOMATOES

*My maternal grandmother Dina was a caring, shy and gentle woman. As children, when we visited her, my cousins and I would play in her vegetable garden with tiny toy pots and pans. I can still recall the stories she told us about the war; some of them were funny, and when she came to those anecdotes, she would start to laugh. It was silent laughter, yet contagious. She was a wonderful cook, especially when it came to wholesome, earthy recipes. The flavour of maltagliati takes me straight back to her garden, her war stories and her quiet, contagious laughter.*

**INGREDIENTS**
*Serves 4*

- 150g (1 cup) cherry tomatoes, ideally in mixed colours
- extra virgin olive oil
- pinch of sugar
- 1 quantity fresh pasta dough (see page 31)
- semolina, for dusting
- 1 garlic clove
- 1 rosemary sprig
- small piece of chilli (optional)
- 200g (1 cup) chickpeas (garbanzo beans), home-cooked or canned, drained
- rosemary or basil leaves (optional)
- salt and freshly ground black pepper

Preheat the oven to 120°C (250°F), Gas Mark ½.

Wash and halve the cherry tomatoes, arranging them cut side up in a baking tray lined with baking paper. Drizzle with olive oil, sprinkle with the sugar, salt and pepper and roast for 1–1½ hours, until caramelized and slightly dried.

Meanwhile, roll out the pasta dough as described on page 31, to a thickness of about 0.5mm (1/32 inch). Cut the fresh pasta sheets into irregular squares (maltagliati means 'badly cut') using a fluted pastry wheel. Dust the pieces with semolina to prevent them from sticking.

In a large frying pan, warm a drizzle of olive oil with the whole garlic clove and rosemary sprig, adding the small piece of chilli for heat, if you like. Lightly toast the aromatics, then add the chickpeas and let them cook for a few minutes.

Meanwhile, bring a pan of salted water to the boil and cook the maltagliati for 2–3 minutes, until they rise to the surface. Keep an eye on the chickpeas, adding a little pasta cooking water to make them creamier. If you like, you can purée a portion of them for a smoother texture.

Drain the pasta and add it to the frying pan with the chickpeas. Toss gently for a minute to blend the flavours. Serve with the confit tomatoes scattered on top, finishing with a drizzle of olive oil, black pepper to taste and, if you wish, a sprinkling of rosemary or basil leaves.

# MATUFFI WITH MUSHROOMS

*Camaiore, though small, contains many different ecosystems and atmospheres, from the seaside at Lido to the mountain huts high in the Apuan Alps. The local cuisine exhibits the same variety, ranging from raw seafood to comforting polenta with mushrooms. In exploring traditional Camaiorese dishes to offer our guests, I came across matuffi, which is usually served with a rich meat ragù. Given the abundance of mushrooms that grow around our farmhouse, this vegetarian version feels especially fitting.*

**INGREDIENTS**
*Serves 4*

- 50g (1¾oz) dried porcini mushrooms
- 3½ tablespoons extra virgin olive oil, plus extra for the polenta
- bunch of parsley, finely chopped
- 2 garlic cloves, crushed
- 1 small chilli
- 30g (2 tablespoons) tomato purée
- 200ml (¾ cup plus 1 tablespoon) tomato passata
- 250g (1¾ cups) polenta (not quick-cook)
- 100g (1 cup) grated Parmesan cheese, or pecorino cheese (ideally Tuscan)
- salt and freshly ground black pepper

Soak the porcini in a bowl of hot water until rehydrated. Once soft, drain and chop them roughly, reserving some of their soaking liquid.

In a large saucepan, warm the olive oil. Add the parsley, garlic and whole chilli, taking care not to let them burn. As soon as the mixture begins to sizzle gently, add the mushrooms. Let them absorb the flavours, then pour in a little of the reserved soaking liquid to deepen the taste.

Stir in the tomato purée and add the passata. Season with salt and pepper and let the sauce simmer.

Meanwhile, bring a pan of salted water with a splash of olive oil to the boil. Slowly pour in the polenta, stirring constantly with a whisk or wooden spoon to prevent lumps from forming. Cook over a medium heat for about 40 minutes, until soft and creamy.

To assemble, spoon a layer of the mushroom sauce into four deep plates or shallow bowls. Using two spoons, form three soft quenelles of polenta and place them on top of the sauce. Pour over an extra spoonful of sauce, allowing it to cascade gently over the polenta. Finish with a generous dusting of grated Parmesan or, for a rustic touch, Tuscan pecorino, and a twist of black pepper to taste.

Alternatively, for a heartier, more traditional presentation, you can layer the dish: spoon some mushroom sauce into the base of a deep plate or shallow bowl, then cover with a portion of polenta. Continue alternating layers of sauce and polenta until all the ingredients are used up. Finish with a dusting of grated cheese and black pepper to taste.

# MINESTRA DI CAVOLFIORE (CAULIFLOWER SOUP)

*This is a traditional soup from Livorno. Curiously, it wasn't Alessandro's father, a true native of Livorno, who first introduced me to his local recipe, but Rossella, my Roman manager and trusted collaborator, who often cooks it. During wartime, cauliflower was an essential source of nourishment in the Italian countryside, so this humble soup – uniting simplicity and history – has become a symbol of resilience and continuity for me.*

**INGREDIENTS**
*Serves 4*

- 1 cauliflower, about 700–800g (1lb 9oz–1lb 12oz)
- 1.5 litres (6 cups) vegetable stock (broth), made using 1½ bouillon cubes
- 1 large onion, about 200g (7oz)
- 1 celery heart, about 250g (9oz)
- extra virgin olive oil
- 30g (2 tablespoons) tomato purée
- 1 small chilli (optional)
- 100g (3½oz) spaghetti, broken
- 50g (½ cup) grated pecorino cheese
- salt and freshly ground black pepper

Wash the cauliflower and remove the outer leaves. Break the head into florets and boil them in a saucepan with the stock.

Meanwhile, finely chop the onion and celery to make a battuto, the Italian aromatic base. Warm some olive oil in a deep pan, then add the chopped vegetables. Sauté until the onion turns golden, then stir in the tomato purée and let it cook with the battuto. If you like, you can add the chilli at this stage (left whole, or chopped for more heat, if you prefer).

Once the cauliflower is tender, lift it out of the stock with a slotted spoon, reserving the cooking liquid, and transfer it to the pan with the sautéed vegetables. Stir well to coat, then break up the cauliflower with the spoon, or with a potato masher. Add the reserved cooking liquid and let it simmer, uncovered, over a low heat.

After about 30 minutes, when the stock has reduced, add the broken spaghetti pieces and stir. When the pasta is cooked (about 10 minutes), serve the soup hot, topped with the pecorino and a twist of black pepper.

# PAPPA COL POMODORO (TUSCAN TOMATO AND BREAD SOUP)

*'Viva la pappa, pappa, pappa, col popo-popo-popo pomodoro!' sang Rita Pavone in the 1960s, and rightly so. This thick Tuscan tomato and bread soup is easy to make, flavourful and deeply comforting. Most importantly, it can feed many with very little, which makes it the perfect dish for village festivals and country fairs. It became a symbol of conviviality and cheer in an Italy that was rising again after years of hardship and war. All you need is bread, garlic and tomatoes (or tomato passata), a sturdy casserole dish (preferably terracotta) and some good music. Your guests will thank you, especially if you serve it while humming Rita's song.*

**INGREDIENTS**
*Serves 4*

- 700g (1lb 9oz) ripe plum tomatoes, or 500g (2 cups) tomato passata
- handful of basil leaves, plus extra to serve
- pinch of granulated sugar
- 500g (1lb 2oz) rustic unsalted bread
- extra virgin olive oil
- 3 garlic cloves
- pinch of chilli flakes
- 1.5 litres (6 cups) vegetable stock (broth)
- salt and freshly ground black pepper

If using tomato passata, skip this step. Otherwise, if tomatoes are in season and you have the time, wash them and place in a saucepan with just enough water to cover. Place a lid on the pan and cook for about 20 minutes, until the tomato skins wrinkle. Drain, then pass them through a food mill to obtain a thin sauce, discarding the skin and seeds. Return your homemade sauce, or the tomato passata, to the saucepan with the basil leaves, sugar and a little salt. Let it simmer for another 20 minutes, until it reaches the desired consistency.

Slice the bread thinly, then break it into smaller pieces by hand.

Cut the garlic into large pieces. Warm some olive oil with the garlic in a large flameproof casserole dish. Let the oil absorb the flavour, then remove the garlic.

Add the chilli flakes to the oil, then stir in the bread so it absorbs the flavour. Warm the stock in a separate pan, then add the tomato sauce to the bread. Stir well so the bread soaks it up. Place over a medium heat and let it simmer, gradually adding stock with a ladle as the mixture thickens.

Allow to cool slightly and serve lukewarm, finished with a drizzle of olive oil, black pepper to taste and a few more basil leaves.

# POTATO LEEK SOUP

*This was perhaps the very first thing I tasted upon arriving in New York. There was a deli, one of those places serving quick and good breakfasts and lunches, that offered a soup-and-bagel combo for less than four dollars. Among the soups on the board there was one called 'French Potato Leek'. Curious because of the 'European twist', I tried it and was immediately won over. I can still remember those freezing winter days and the comfort of sipping that warm, velvety soup from a cup after walking the icy city streets.*

**INGREDIENTS**
*Serves 4*

- 4 leeks
- 100g (7 tablespoons) unsalted butter
- 3 garlic cloves, finely chopped
- 1 thyme sprig
- 1kg (2lb 4oz) potatoes
- 1 litre (4 cups) vegetable stock (broth)
- salt and freshly ground black pepper

*To serve (optional, but recommended)*

- crumbled feta cheese
- extra virgin olive oil

Clean and slice the leeks thinly, then place them in a deep saucepan. Add the butter and melt it over a medium-high heat, stirring it with the leeks and letting them soften. Add the garlic and thyme, continuing to stir so the aromatics infuse the butter.

Peel and cut the potatoes into small chunks. Once the leeks are tender and wilted, add the potatoes, stir well, then cover with the vegetable stock. Adjust the seasoning with salt, reduce the heat, then cover, letting the soup cook gently for about 30 minutes.

When the potatoes are soft, remove the thyme stalk and blitz the mixture with a food processor or hand blender until smooth and creamy. The traditional recipe calls for adding cream, but I prefer to lighten it with a splash of water to keep the soup fluid and delicate.

Serve hot in deep bowls, finished with a twist of freshly ground black pepper and scattered with crumbled feta and olive oil, if you like.

# SKILLET EGGS WITH NEW POTATOES AND SPINACH

*More than just a side dish, this is a tribute to American diners, where potatoes are seared on a griddle until crisp. To give the dish an Italian touch, I decided to enrich it with Parmesan and spinach. It takes me back to when my friend Javonne and I worked as porters at the W Hotel in New York. At the end of our shifts, we would dash to the nearest diner for a well-earned meal. There, over an omelette and these delicious potatoes, we shared stories and made plans for our futures.*

**INGREDIENTS**
*Serves 4*

- 400g (14oz) new potatoes
- 1 tablespoon extra virgin olive oil
- 200g (7oz) mixed mushrooms
- 1 garlic clove
- 100g (3½oz) baby spinach
- 2–4 eggs
- generous pinch of chilli flakes
- 4 tablespoons grated Parmesan cheese (optional)
- salt

Preheat the oven to 200°C (400°F), Gas Mark 6.

Cut the potatoes into chunks or coins about 2–3cm (1 inch) thick. Place them in an ovenproof pan – I like to use a heavy, cast-iron frying pan for this – drizzle with the olive oil, season with salt and roast for 15 minutes.

Quarter the mushrooms and finely chop the garlic, then add them to the potatoes and toss everything together. Return the pan to the oven for another 10 minutes, until the potatoes are tender.

Remove from the oven and stir in the spinach, letting it wilt in the heat of the pan. With the back of a spoon, make 2 or 4 small wells in the vegetables and crack the eggs into them. Season with salt and chilli flakes.

If you like, sprinkle Parmesan on top for a rich, savoury finish. Return the pan to the oven and bake for 6–8 minutes, until the eggs are just set.

# CIAMBELLONE (ITALIAN RING CAKE)

*When we were kids in Tuscany, there was a tradition of being 'healed'. Every year, my mother would take us four to visit my great-aunt Giovanna, who always welcomed us with ciambellone cake, bread and Nutella. Then, one by one, my great-aunt would take us into the garden, where we sat on a chair while she performed ablutions on our legs, arms and faces with a cloth dipped into a basin of water and recited prayers. I still remember the scent of ironwort, also called the 'herb of fear', which was infused in the water for these rituals, mingling with the fragrance of the cake and the scent of the flowers in the garden. In my region of Tuscany, the traditional ciambellone Versilia pan was created: a special vessel that allows the cake to be baked on the hob rather than in the oven.*

**INGREDIENTS**
*Serves 4*

- 110g (½ cup) butter, plus extra for the tin
- 4 eggs
- 250g (1¼ cups) caster (superfine) sugar
- 140ml (½ cup plus 2 tablespoons) milk
- 300g (2½ cups) plain flour, plus extra for the tin
- finely grated zest of 1 lemon, or 1 teaspoon vanilla extract
- 1 tablespoon baking powder
- salt
- icing (powdered) sugar, for dusting (optional)

Melt and cool the butter. Separate the eggs, letting the whites reach room temperature. Whip the whites into stiff peaks with a pinch of salt and set aside.

Separately beat the yolks with an electric mixer until foamy, then gradually add the sugar, continuing to whisk until the mixture is pale and fluffy. Incorporate the melted cooled butter, then slowly add the milk, giving the batter time to absorb it completely.

Add the dry ingredients next, sifting in the flour a little at a time so it blends evenly. For a richer flavour, add the lemon zest or vanilla. Gently fold in the baking powder, whisking briefly to combine. Finally, delicately fold in the beaten egg whites, moving your spoon from the bottom to the top of the bowl to avoid deflating them.

Preheat the oven to 180°C (350°F), Gas Mark 4. Butter and flour a ring cake tin, pour in the batter and bake on the middle shelf for about 40 minutes. Test with a skewer to check if it's cooked through: the skewer should come out clean.

Let the ciambellone cool slightly before taking it out of the tin. Dust with icing sugar, if you like. The cake keeps well for 3–4 days in an airtight container.

# GÂTEAU MONT BLANC

*While I was working as a television correspondent during the pandemic, I found myself in Courmayeur in northern Italy, staying in a beautiful hotel entirely buried under the snow. At dinner, I was the only guest in the dining room. The chef spoiled me, and at the end of the meal he brought me a special gâteau Mont Blanc, made with boiled chestnuts. In winter, I always recreate this recipe at our farmhouse. I find it a true delight.*

**INGREDIENTS**
*Serves 4*

- 200g (1 cup) caster (superfine) sugar
- 50ml (3 tablespoons) boiling water
- 200g (1½ cups) cooked chestnuts
- 300ml (1¼ cups) double (heavy) cream
- 100g (3½oz) meringues

To make the caramel, melt the sugar in a heavy-based saucepan over a medium heat. Do not stir until it has turned golden and fully liquefied.

Carefully add the boiling water, whisking immediately to prevent lumps. Take care, as hot caramel may splatter. Continue whisking until you have a smooth sauce with a glossy consistency.

Dip the chestnuts into the caramel, coating them gently. Transfer to a sheet of baking paper to cool.

In a bowl, whip the cream until soft and slightly thickened: it should hold its shape, but not be too stiff. (There's no need to chill the bowl in advance for this, as the cream should remain soft rather than overly firm.)

Spread a layer of whipped cream on a serving platter. Crumble the meringues evenly over it. Scatter the caramelized chestnuts on top. Make sure the remaining caramel is neither too runny nor too thick for the perfect texture, then, with a spoon, drizzle it over the dessert to finish.

The whipped cream should be light and airy, providing a contrast to the crunch of the meringues and the sweetness of the caramelized chestnuts.

## MUSIC,
### *a Nostalgic Journey*

Music has been a constant companion in my life, the invisible thread binding every moment, every emotion, every journey. Since childhood, I have used music to create a safe space, an atmosphere that allows my inner life, my emotions, to exist. For me, music opens the door to introspection and communication; it is an emotional catalyst. Decades may pass since I last heard it, yet the first notes of a particular song can unlock a memory, a sensation that awakens all my senses.

For me, music is also a family bond. I remember long car rides with my father when he travelled north to visit clients for his textile mill. We played his cassettes of Adriano Celentano, alternated with mine of Rondò Veneziano. When I moved to New York, my musical horizons expanded. In Manhattan, I was exposed to sounds and styles entirely new to me. Italian music, in turn, took on a deeper meaning, nostalgia imbuing certain songs with a greater intensity and tenderness.

At Le Gusciane, I dedicate a moment each day to listening freely, exploring new sounds. It is a way of adding to the playlists that accompany life at the farmhouse, from the rising of the sun to the dimming of the last bedside lamp. Our mornings always begin with soothing tunes. I gravitate towards contemporary composers, such as Ludovico Einaudi, neoclassical pianists such as George Winston and James Quinn, as well as film scores. This atmosphere allows me to start the day in calmness and serenity, without diving immediately into my to-do list.

As the day unfolds, my tastes shift, ranging from folk singers to pop, especially when I'm travelling by car. But at home, it is the legends of jazz – Ella Fitzgerald, Peggy Lee, Billie Holiday – who most often fill the air. Soul too, especially the voice of Roberta Flack, will drift through the rooms. I am drawn to soft voices and muffled atmospheres, especially on those afternoons when the farmhouse itself seems to be dozing in the embrace of the valley.

When the sun begins to dip behind the horizon, it's the jazz of Miles Davis and John Coltrane that creates a sensual, magical and captivating atmosphere. This is the soundtrack that accompanies me almost every time I'm in the kitchen. For example, when my daughter was little, she knew that as soon as *Kind of Blue* started playing, it meant that I had my hands in the dough, making pizza.

In New York, I also discovered fado, a haunting music born in the Portuguese-African colonies to express *saudade*, that deep sense of longing for a distant homeland. The magic of fado is perfect for our farmhouse, so it too is an essential part of my playlist.

For Latin music, I have to thank Tanti Baci, the small basement restaurant in the Village in New York, where I heard a wide variety of musical styles. Most of the kitchen staff were South American, so the Latin rhythms of Julio Iglesias, Gloria Estefan and the Buena Vista Social Club were an integral part of our daily soundtrack. Even though years have gone by, today, when I cook dinner, I still like to soak in the ambience created by those sounds. I love recreating that *barrio* atmosphere around me, as if the kitchen of Le Gusciane were transformed into that of Tanti Baci. And the music means that every evening becomes a celebration.

*The magic of fado feels made for the farmhouse; it instantly became an essential part of my playlist.*

# WINTER

*The mists roll in and everything seems to pause, as if nature itself is taking a deep breath. The light softens. At our farmhouse, the stoves are lit and food warms the soul.*

Winter days at the farmhouse carry a charm all of their own. The season has the power to transform the landscape into a living canvas, where the silvery greys of the fog mingle with the golden warmth of the winter sun. The pale morning light spreads slowly, revealing the fields in front of the house. The lawn, frosted by the night, shimmers like a cloak of crystal under the shy rays of the sun breaking through the clouds. Behind the farmhouse, the woods lie bare and hushed, gradually filling with light as sunbeams slip between the branches. It is as though the forest is quietly revealing its secrets.

*At the farmhouse, each season arrives with its own music. In winter, the voices of Ella Fitzgerald, Peggy Lee and Billie Holiday take centre stage. Their voices carry a kind of magic, the power to awaken deep emotions. When the notes of 'Have You Met Miss Jones?' or 'Let's Do It' fill the air, it feels as if the music itself comes alive.*

Winter light is unlike any other. Soft and golden, it turns the grey mist into silver sparkles. And when the fog lifts from the mountains, the peaks of Prana, Gabberi and Matanna reveal their snowy crowns. It is a breathtaking sight, binding the farmhouse even more deeply to the majesty of the mountains that rise above it.

Every corner of Le Gusciane becomes part of this dance of colours. The windows transform into paintings that capture the ever-shifting landscape; even the interiors mirror winter's palette. Fabrics and woodwork within blend with the shades of grey and gold outside, creating harmony between indoors and out.

Winter in the countryside has taught me that beauty can be found even in the most delicate hues, the most subdued tones. For me, it is an invitation to pause, to contemplate the world through fresh eyes, to rediscover magic in the most simple of details.

Alessandro is always the first to get up on winter mornings. Calmly, he begins his daily rituals: collecting fresh eggs from the henhouse; stacking wood for the cast-iron stoves and fireplaces.

Meanwhile, our dachshunds, always eager for warmth on the coldest days, curl up together in their bed by the fire. Little balls of fur, they peek at us with curious eyes as we move through our daily routines, as if they carry within them some innate wisdom. It is impossible to resist their charm.

Winter days at the farmhouse are a return to life's simplest things, an invitation to slow down and savour the quiet beauty of the everyday.

IL PLEDDINO

# CHICKPEAS WITH CABBAGE AND KALE

*One of the very first dishes born at Le Gusciane, this remains the recipe that earns us the most compliments. It all began during a Sunday lunch cooked with Rosalba, Alessandro's mother, while we were still in the middle of the renovation work. We had practically nothing in the larder apart from a head of Savoy cabbage and a few jars of chickpeas (garbanzo beans). I remember how we ate them with great appetite at a makeshift table, with slices of toasted bread drizzled in olive oil. Over time, the recipe evolved and has since become one of the cornerstones of our menu.*

INGREDIENTS
*Serves 4*

- 250g (1¼ cups) dried chickpeas (garbanzo beans) or 500g (2½ cups) cooked chickpeas
- 4 leaves cavolo nero or Savoy cabbage
- extra virgin olive oil
- 2 garlic cloves, crushed
- ½ tablespoon chilli flakes
- 1 tablespoon tomato purée
- salt

If you have the time, start with dried chickpeas: rinse them well and soak for 12 hours, changing the water a couple of times. Drain and rinse thoroughly to remove impurities. Cover with fresh water in a large saucepan – or, better still, a traditional terracotta pot, if you happen to have one – and simmer gently for about 1 hour. (A pressure cooker works too, if you're in a hurry.) Never add salt during this stage, as it toughens the skins and prolongs the cooking time; properly cooked chickpeas should melt in your mouth.

If you're short of time – as I often am – ready-cooked chickpeas are perfectly fine. I prefer those sold in glass jars, as I find the larger chickpeas creamier than those in cans.

Prepare your cabbage: in winter I use cavolo nero, in summer Savoy cabbage. Wash the leaves, remove the tough central ribs, and cut them into pieces; I prefer not to chop them too finely.

In a large, deep pan (I like to use a big nonstick wok), warm some olive oil and add the crushed garlic. As soon as the oil is hot, add the cabbage and cover with a lid. When the cabbage begins to wilt, remove the lid, add the chilli flakes, and sauté until lightly toasted.

At this point, add the chickpeas with a little of their cooking liquid (reserve the rest to add later if the dish becomes too dry). Season with salt and stir in the tomato purée, then cover and reduce the heat.

Once the chickpeas begin to break down, purée about one-third of them directly in the pan with a hand blender, stirring well to combine. Use a spatula to scrape up the flavourful crust that forms along the edges of the pan. Serve hot, ideally with toasted bread.

# PUNTARELLE MILLEFOGLIE

*During my time living in Rome, while working as a keyholder welcoming tourists to their holiday apartments, I often found myself in Trastevere, waiting for guests to arrive. That's where I discovered Da Teo, a trattoria that quickly became one of my favourites. Teo, with his boundless creativity in the kitchen, and Tiziana, with her joyful hospitality, ran the place with a truly special touch.*

*Puntarelle is an elongated variant of chicory that is particularly associated with Rome, and this dish – one of Teo's – was a delight I often treated myself to during those long hours of waiting. It's a recipe that has always made me feel deeply connected to the life of the city.*

*If you cannot find Sardinian flatbread (pane carasau), you can substitute flour tortillas. Brush them with olive oil and a pinch of salt, bake until crisp, then break into pieces.*

INGREDIENTS

*Serves 4*

- 1 teaspoon miso paste
- 4 tablespoons extra virgin olive oil, plus extra for brushing
- 2 tablespoons apple cider vinegar
- 1 garlic clove
- 400g (14oz) puntarelle (see introduction above)
- juice of ½ lemon
- 1 burrata cheese, about 150g (5½oz)
- 100g (scant ½ cup) soft goats' cheese
- 200g (7oz) pane carasau (Sardinian flatbread)
- freshly ground black pepper

In a bowl, whisk together the miso paste, olive oil and vinegar. Crush the garlic and let it rest in the dressing to infuse its flavour; the saltiness of the miso should be enough for seasoning.

Preheat the oven to 220°C (425°F), Gas Mark 7.

Wash and clean the puntarelle. To obtain the traditional curls, trim the base and separate each sprout, discarding the tougher parts and outer leaves (these can be set aside to add later if you like). Slice each sprout in half lengthways, then cut each half into thin strips. Immediately place the strips in iced water with the lemon juice.

Meanwhile, prepare the cheese mix, blending the creamy part of the burrata with the goats' cheese until smooth. Brush the pane carasau with olive oil and bake for 10 minutes, until crisp.

Pat the puntarelle dry with kitchen paper.

Assemble the dish by alternating layers of puntarelle, cheese mix and flatbread, seasoning with pepper as you go. You can plate it in a classic millefoglie stack, or play with other compositions; the important thing is to serve it right away, so the flatbread stays crisp.

# TUSCAN RUSTIC CAESAR SALAD

*The first time I tasted Caesar salad was in San Francisco, on one of my earliest business trips. Being Italian, I was taken by my colleagues to a true 'family-style' restaurant, where the portions were enormous. I still remember the looks on everyone's faces around the table as they asked me about the origins of this salad, and I – just as surprised as they were – had to disclose that Caesar salad was not part of our culinary tradition. That evening stayed with me, not only for the discovery of a new dish, but also for the joy of sharing time together under the San Francisco sky.*

**INGREDIENTS**
*Serves 4*

- 1 bunch of cavolo nero
- 1 Delicata squash, or similar firm pumpkin
- 3 tablespoons extra virgin olive oil, plus extra for brushing and (optional) to serve
- 2 slices of rustic country bread
- 3 tablespoons flaked almonds, toasted
- 2 tablespoons panko crumbs
- 50g (½ cup) grated Parmesan cheese, plus extra to serve
- salt and freshly ground black pepper

*For the dressing*

- 225g (1 cup) mayonnaise
- 2 tablespoons Dijon mustard
- 3 tablespoons lemon juice

Wash the cavolo nero thoroughly, remove the tough ribs and chop the leaves into small pieces.

Preheat the oven to 200°C (400°F), Gas Mark 6.

Wash and slice the squash, discarding the seeds, and cut into thin wedges. The skin is edible and delicious, so leave it on. Arrange the slices on a baking sheet lined with baking paper. Brush with some extra olive oil and season with a pinch of salt and pepper, making sure the slices are evenly coated. Roast for 20–25 minutes, turning halfway through, until tender and golden. Allow to cool slightly.

Prepare the bread by cutting it into cubes, tossing with the measured olive oil, plus salt and pepper. Toast in the oven for about 10 minutes, until crisp.

For the dressing, whisk the mayonnaise, Dijon mustard and lemon juice together in a bowl until smooth and creamy.

Put the chopped cavolo nero in a large bowl, pour the dressing over and massage it into the leaves. Add the roasted squash, toasted croutons, flaked almonds, panko, salt, pepper and Parmesan. Toss well to ensure everything is evenly coated. Let the salad rest for a few minutes to allow the flavours to meld.

Plate the salad, finishing by shaving over extra Parmesan and, if you like, a final drizzle of olive oil.

# BRAISED FENNEL WITH RAISINS, PINE NUTS AND OLIVES

*In my first two years living in Rome, I shared an apartment with Michele, an aspiring actor and screenwriter from Milan, who had a particular gift for improvising in the kitchen. This recipe, one of his favourites, always felt like a small performance: fennel and pine nuts dancing together in a wintry symphony that filled our home with warmth and fragrance. For Michele, cooking was like acting: a way to express creativity and unforgettable emotion.*

INGREDIENTS

*Serves 4*

- 100g (¾ cup) raisins
- 4 fennel bulbs
- 30g (1oz) butter
- 50g (⅓ cup) pine nuts
- 2 tablespoons vinegar, apple cider or white wine, as preferred
- 1 tablespoon sugar
- 100g (½ cup) pitted Taggiasca olives, or other small black olives
- salt and freshly ground black pepper

Soak the raisins in a bowl of warm water to make them plump.

Clean the fennel by removing the fibrous outer layers, then cut each bulb into 8 lengthways wedges. Bring a saucepan of water to the boil and blanch the fennel for a few minutes, until just tender, then drain and pat dry thoroughly.

In a frying pan, melt the butter and arrange the fennel wedges in it, browning them for about 30 seconds on each side. Season with salt and pepper.

Meanwhile, in a separate dry pan, lightly toast the pine nuts until golden brown.

Once the fennel has taken on a golden colour on both sides, add the vinegar and sugar, letting it cook for a few more minutes.

Stir in the olives, toasted pine nuts and drained raisins, cooking a little longer and stirring occasionally so the fennel absorbs all the flavours evenly.

Serve warm, to enjoy the full harmony of flavours that meld together during cooking.

# BUTTERNUT SQUASH AND RADICCHIO CASSEROLE

*I first met Alessia, a television writer, during what was supposed to be an audition, and we immediately hit it off. That same spark continued during filming and a beautiful friendship was born, filled with shared confidences, laughter and the exchange of good advice. Alessia is multifaceted and sporty, a long-time yoga teacher and endlessly curious about discovering new things, places and dishes. Our mutual spirit of experimentation often leads us to test new culinary creations. Beyond eating the results, these are always occasions to spend time together and dive into wonderful, meaningful conversations.*

INGREDIENTS
*Serves 4*

- 100g (¾ cup) cashew nuts
- 3 tablespoons extra virgin olive oil, plus extra for brushing
- 85g (¼ cup) finely chopped red onion
- 1 small butternut squash, peeled, deseeded and diced
- 2 teaspoons finely chopped rosemary leaves
- 1 teaspoon sea salt, plus extra for seasoning
- 60ml (¼ cup) white wine
- juice of 1 lemon
- ½ head of red radicchio, finely chopped
- rustic bread, to serve

Soak the cashews in water for 2–3 hours before you begin, making sure they are well submerged.

Warm the olive oil in a large, heavy-based pan over a medium heat. Add the onion and cook until translucent, about 1 minute. Add the squash, rosemary and salt, stirring well. Partially cover the pan and cook until the squash begins to soften and break down, 5–7 minutes, adding a few tablespoons of water if the pan looks dry.

Pour in the white wine and let it simmer, scraping up any bits from the bottom of the pan. Once the wine has been absorbed, remove from the heat, cover and leave to rest for 5 minutes.

Preheat the oven to 200°C (400°F), Gas Mark 6.

Drain the cashews and blend them with the lemon juice until smooth. Season with salt to taste. In a large bowl, combine the cashew cream with the squash mixture and the finely chopped radicchio.

Transfer half the mixture to a food processor, blend until creamy, then fold it back into the remaining mixture. Spoon everything into a baking dish or cast-iron pan and bake until golden on top. This will take 15–20 minutes.

Leave to rest for 5 minutes while you toast the bread slices and brush them with olive oil. Serve the toasts with the casserole.

# GLAZED BRUSSELS SPROUTS

*I discovered this recipe at one of my favourite restaurants in Los Angeles, and it completely changed my mind about these little spheres, which I had previously regarded with suspicion. Glazed Brussels sprouts turn out to be delicious and flavourful, with a pleasing texture and a truly distinctive, sophisticated taste. This is one of Alessandro's favourite dishes – in fact, I always make a couple of extra servings because I know he won't be able to stop eating them.*

**INGREDIENTS**
*Serves 4*

- 350g (12oz) Brussels sprouts
- 100 ml (½ cup) extra virgin olive oil
- 60g (¼ cup) miso paste
- 1½ tablespoon apple cider vinegar
- 45g (¼ cup) agave syrup or acacia honey
- 1 teaspoon soy sauce or tamari

Preheat the oven to 220°C (425°F), Gas Mark 7.

Wash the Brussels sprouts, trim the bases, remove the outer leaves and cut them in half. Pat them thoroughly dry with kitchen paper.

In a tall, narrow container, combine the olive oil and miso paste, then add the apple cider vinegar, agave syrup and soy sauce. Purée with a hand blender until smooth and viscous.

Line a baking dish with baking paper, making sure it extends up the sides. Place the cleaned, dried sprouts inside and coat them with the glaze, either massaging it in with your hands or using a silicone brush to ensure they are evenly covered.

Bake for about 30 minutes. Once the sprouts begin to caramelize, turn them with a spatula and move the dish to the top oven shelf, switching on the grill for an additional 5 minutes.

Allow to cool slightly before serving in a large bowl or small individual cups.

# ROASTED ROMANESCO WITH YOGURT AND STRACCIATELLA

*I have always admired the culinary talents of my friend Andrea Provvidenza. For a time, I lived with him in Rome, and every evening he would conjure up delicious dishes with an ease that never ceased to amaze me. I remember our trips to the market: Andrea would flirt with all the sellers, while tasting and selecting only the very best ingredients. It's no surprise that he has friends from all over the world who come to visit him, eager to be enchanted both by his charm and by his excellent cooking.*

INGREDIENTS
*Serves 4*

- ½ head of cauliflower
- ½ head of Romanesco broccoli
- extra virgin olive oil
- 1 tablespoon apple cider vinegar, plus 1 tablespoon extra for dressing
- chilli flakes
- 2 sweet potatoes
- 200g (¾ cup) Greek yogurt
- 200g (7oz) stracciatella cheese
- thyme leaves
- 30g (¼ cup) sunflower seeds
- 20g (scant ¼ cup) pumpkin seeds
- 50g (⅓ cup) cashew nuts
- salt and freshly ground black pepper

Preheat the oven to 180°C (350°F), Gas Mark 4.

Wash the cauliflower and cut into 1cm (½ inch) slices. Arrange on a baking sheet lined with baking paper. Separate the Romanesco florets, halving the larger ones, and add them to the same tray. Brush with olive oil, coating all sides, and season with salt.

In a small bowl, mix 2 tablespoons of olive oil with the vinegar, a pinch of chilli flakes and a little salt.

Scrub the sweet potatoes well to remove any soil or root hairs. Slice into 2cm (¾-inch) rounds, dip briefly in the chilli dressing and arrange on a separate baking sheet. Bake the sweet potatoes, cauliflower and Romanesco for about 30 minutes.

Meanwhile, mix the Greek yogurt with the stracciatella in a bowl. Add a pinch of thyme and season with salt, to taste. When the Romanesco and cauliflower are crisping at the edges and the sweet potatoes are starting to caramelize, remove both trays from the oven and cool for 5 minutes.

To serve, spread a layer of the yogurt cream on the plate, then arrange the roasted vegetables on top. Chop the seeds and cashews and sprinkle them over.

Prepare a light vinaigrette to serve on the side, for anyone who might like it, by mixing together 2 tablespoons of olive oil, 1 tablespoon of apple cider vinegar, a pinch of salt and some freshly ground pepper.

STAUB
STAUB
STAUB

# INCAVOLATA CAMAIORESE

*In the course of the many errands I had to run during the renovation work on our farmhouse, I had the chance to meet the then-mayor of Camaiore. Alessandro del Dotto is a capable and kind young man who, over the years, has become a friend. It feels only right to dedicate one of the emblematic dishes of our valley to him. The people of Camaiore are very proud, but this doesn't diminish their playful Tuscan spirit, so incavolato (which means both 'angry' and 'full of cabbage') suits them perfectly! This rustic farinata takes its name from the black kale grown in the fields of Capezzano Pianore, a patch of countryside that separates Camaiore from its seaside Lido.*

*The secret to this recipe is planning ahead, because in addition to the beans, you need their cooking liquid, which is essential. In my hometown of Prato, every bakery sells its own beans cooked overnight, so they're easy to find. If you don't have the good fortune to have a Tuscan bakery nearby, you'll need to prepare your own beans in advance.*

**INGREDIENTS**
*Serves 4*

- 150g (⅔ cup) dried borlotti beans or 300g (1½ cups) cooked borlotti beans
- 2 garlic cloves
- 1½ onions
- 1½ carrots
- 3 celery sticks
- a few sage sprigs
- a few parsley sprigs
- extra virgin olive oil
- 120ml (½ cup) tomato passata
- 700ml (3 cups) vegetable stock (broth)
- 150g (5½oz) cavolo nero
- 200g (1½ cups) polenta (not quick-cook)
- salt and freshly ground black pepper

Soak the dried beans in cold water for 12 hours. Halve 1 garlic clove, 1 onion, 1 carrot and 2 celery sticks, place in a saucepan with the drained beans and cover with fresh water. Cook over a low heat for 2 hours. Once cooked, drain, reserving some of the cooking liquid and remove the vegetables. Pass half the beans through a food mill and return them to their cooking water. Set the remaining whole beans aside.

Finely chop 1 small celery stick, the remaining garlic clove, ½ carrot, ½ small onion and a few leaves of sage and parsley. Sauté these aromatics in a generous amount of olive oil in a large saucepan. When the onion turns translucent, add the passata thinned with a glass of the stock. Once it begins to boil, add the puréed beans with their cooking liquid. Bring everything back to the boil.

Prepare the cavolo nero by removing the tough stems and slicing the leaves into strips. Add to the saucepan and cook for about 30 minutes, stirring occasionally and adding ladles of the remaining stock if the mixture thickens too much. Season with salt and pepper.

Add most of the reserved whole beans, then sift in the polenta gradually, stirring continuously to avoid lumps and prevent sticking. Cook for a further 20 minutes or so, until the soup has the consistency of a soft polenta. Adjust the seasoning, remove from the heat and leave to rest a little before serving with the remaining whole beans and a drizzle of olive oil.

# PASTA E FAGIOLI

*A recipe that instantly evokes the warmth of home, this version of the classic Italian dish was taught to me by my friend Diego, who is a shoe designer and a true Neapolitan. He invited me over for dinner one evening; I had been staying in Milan, shooting a television show, and after a long stretch of restaurants and room service, a home-cooked dinner was exactly what I needed. Pasta e fagioli is like the embrace of a friend: with the very first spoonful, you immediately realize how much you missed them.*

*This dish is wonderful reheated the next day, when it becomes ripassata. To make that, add a little water, olive oil and grated Parmesan and warm the soup gently. When it begins to form a crust, toss it in the pan before serving.*

**INGREDIENTS**
*Serves 4*

- 500g (2¼ cups) dried cannellini beans, or 2 × 570g (1lb 4oz) jars of cannellini beans
- bicarbonate of soda, if using dried beans
- 1 carrot
- 1 celery stick
- 1 onion
- extra virgin olive oil
- 300g (10½oz) mezze maniche or ditali pasta
- 1 tablespoon tomato purée
- grated Parmesan cheese
- salt and freshly ground black pepper

If using dried beans, soak them overnight with a pinch of bicarbonate of soda. But if you're in a hurry – as I often am – 2 jars of pre-cooked cannellini beans work perfectly. I prefer those sold in glass jars, so I can see the product. Check if your pre-cooked beans are salted, and if they are, don't add salt until you add the pasta.

Finely chop the carrot, celery and onion, then sauté them in a generous splash of olive oil. As soon as the onion begins to colour, add the drained beans and stir well. Pour in half a glass of water, cover and simmer gently for 40 minutes, or until the cannellini beans are tender. If using pre-cooked beans, add them to the saucepan once the carrot pieces are tender; they won't require further cooking.

Meanwhile, bring some water to the boil in a saucepan.

When the carrot pieces have softened, remove one-third of the beans and purée them with a hand blender until you have a thick cream.

Add the dry pasta to the bean saucepan along with a little of the boiling water. Stir in the blended beans and the tomato purée and, if necessary, a pinch of salt. The soup should not become too thick, so add more boiling water as needed, stirring with a ladle to blend everything together. Continue cooking and stirring until the pasta is tender.

Serve with grated Parmesan, a drizzle of olive oil and freshly ground black pepper.

# BRUSSELS SPROUT AND POMEGRANATE SALAD

*This recipe comes from London, from a lunch at the home of my Brazilian friend Warly, who had moved to the city to be close to her son while he studied in the UK. She was passionate about cookbooks and never missed the chance to buy a new one. From one of those books (by Jamie Oliver) came a dish I found truly enlightening. Even though I've made a few small changes to it, this recipe still has the flavour of Warly's London culinary discovery.*

INGREDIENTS
*Serves 4*

- 500g (1lb 2oz) Brussels sprouts
- 50 g (⅓ cup) shelled unsalted pistachios
- 2 garlic cloves
- extra virgin olive oil
- 1 pomegranate
- 200g (¾ cup) ricotta cheese
- 200g (¾ cup) Greek yogurt
- balsamic vinegar
- salt and freshly ground black pepper

Rinse the Brussels sprouts. Slice them in half and place cut-side down in a nonstick frying pan. Set over a medium-high heat to colour only the cut sides.

Crush the pistachios. Finely chop the garlic. Add the garlic to the sprouts, keeping them cut-side down but stirring the garlic around. Drizzle with a little olive oil and add a splash of water. Cover and cook until the sprouts are tender, then remove from the heat.

Extract the juice from most of the pomegranate seeds, crushing some of them but keeping a handful whole to use later. Strain to collect the juice.

Drain the ricotta and mix it in a bowl with the Greek yogurt, seasoning with salt. Spread this mixture on a serving plate and arrange the Brussels sprouts on top.

Sprinkle with the crushed pistachios, drizzle with the pomegranate juice and scatter over the reserved pomegranate seeds. Finish with a little olive oil, a dash of balsamic vinegar and a twist of black pepper.

# MINESTRA DI PANE (TUSCAN BREAD SOUP)

*Ribollita, which we call minestra di pane in Prato, is the dish that most reminds me of my grandmother Dina. I can recall how its aroma still filled the whole house. It's a humble, nourishing dish that, as she used to say, 'Only comes out right if you make plenty of it.' So call your friends over for dinner, or get lots of containers ready to share it with relatives and neighbours, because when you make this dish, the whole neighbourhood eats it! If you can't find Tuscan unsalted bread, use a rustic country loaf with a dense crumb. Nonna Dina cooked her soup with a ham bone, but this fully vegetarian version is just as delicious.*

INGREDIENTS
*Serves 4*

- 1kg (2lb 4oz) potatoes
- 1kg (2lb 4oz) carrots
- 1kg (2lb 4oz) onions
- 4 courgettes
- 1 celery heart
- 1 bunch of chard
- 2 cavolo nero leaves
- ½ white cabbage
- ½ Savoy cabbage
- extra virgin olive oil
- 750g (3½ cups) cooked borlotti beans
- 1kg (4 cups) cooked cannellini beans
- 2 tablespoons tomato purée
- 1kg (2lb 4oz) unsalted Tuscan bread (see introduction above)
- chilli flakes (optional)
- salt

Wash the vegetables thoroughly. Peel and dice the potatoes, then do the same with the carrots, onions and courgettes. Slice the celery into rounds.

Remove the stems from the chard and cavolo nero. Chop the chard leaves coarsely and set aside. Chop the cavolo nero leaves and the cabbages and place them in a bowl.

In a large saucepan, warm some olive oil and sauté the carrots, onions and celery until well softened. Add the chopped greens from the bowl, stirring well – this step is important, as they need to absorb the flavour of the soffritto vegetables. Cook, stirring often, for about 10 minutes.

Add the potatoes and courgettes, followed by the chard. Cover the pan and cook for a few more minutes.

Purée half each of the borlotti and cannellini beans and add to the saucepan along with the whole beans. Mix well and add enough water to cover the vegetables. When the soup comes to the boil, season with salt and stir in the tomato purée. Cover and simmer gently for 1–1½ hours, stirring occasionally.

Once the potatoes and carrots are tender, remove from the heat. In a separate wide saucepan, begin layering: ladle in some soup, cover with thin slices of bread, and repeat until the pan is full. Cover and let it rest to cool slightly.

The soup is best eaten warm, drizzled with olive oil. If enjoying this the following day, reheat it in a pan (*ribollita* means 'reboiled'), perhaps with a pinch of chilli flakes for extra flavour.

# GNUDI (TUSCAN SPINACH AND RICOTTA DUMPLINGS)

*Although I'm Tuscan, I first discovered gnudi in New York, thanks to my friend Franco D'Alessandro, a playwright and director who had cast me in a stage production about the friendship between the actress Anna Magnani and the writer Tennessee Williams. I remember studying countless interviews with Magnani. In one of them, there was an anecdote about how she was extremely fond of the gnudi made by the film director Franco Zeffirelli's housekeeper. It seems that, one evening, Anna was at his home when Maria Callas arrived. Zeffirelli was very anxious about sparks flying when the two divas met each other, but in fact they ignored him completely, spent the night chatting and polished off two trays of gnudi. Incredible!*

INGREDIENTS
*Serves 4*

*For the gnudi*

- 400g (14oz) fresh spinach
- 250g (1 cup) sheep's milk ricotta cheese, well drained
- 1 large egg
- 100g (1 cup) grated Parmesan cheese, plus extra (optional) to serve
- freshly grated nutmeg
- 85g (½ cup) potato flour, plus extra for dusting
- salt and freshly ground black pepper

*For the sauce*

- extra virgin olive oil
- 200g (7oz) cherry tomatoes, ideally red and yellow
- handful of basil or parsley leaves

Wash the spinach and cook briefly in a pan with a little water until just wilted. Drain and squeeze well to remove as much liquid as possible, then chop finely.

In a bowl, combine the spinach with the drained ricotta, egg, Parmesan, nutmeg, salt and pepper. Stir until you have a smooth, uniform dough.

Add the potato flour gradually, stirring it in, until the mixture is firm enough to shape without sticking to your hands. Lightly dust a tray with potato flour. Scoop up small portions of the mixture and roll into balls about the size of a walnut, or, if you're feeling brave, form quenelles of the mixture instead. Roll the gnudi in flour to prevent them from sticking during cooking.

Cook the gnudi in salted boiling water. When they rise to the surface (after 3–4 minutes), they are ready. Remove with a slotted spoon, keeping them moist with a little of their cooking water and reserving the remainder of the water.

Cut the cherry tomatoes in half. In a pan, warm some olive oil and cook the tomatoes until they begin to burst, then season with salt. Tear in the basil or parsley leaves and add a splash of the gnudi cooking water to create a light emulsion.

Serve the gnudi hot, topped with the tomato sauce, finished with a drizzle of olive oil and some freshly ground black pepper, and, if you like, an extra sprinkling of Parmesan.

# CHIARA'S CHEESECAKE

*Chiara is one of those people who lights up a room. Lively and extroverted, she's impossible to miss. With her strong personality, endless opinions and hilarious stories, she's always the centre of attention. She has been Alessandro's best friend since their teenage years; she's like a sister to him and their bond is unbreakable. Chiara has always had a passion for cooking. When Alessandro and I began thinking about the menus for Le Gusciane, we knew we couldn't leave out her cheesecake. Instead of the classic digestive biscuits, Chiara uses Campagnole, a rustic Italian breakfast biscuit, for the base, which makes her cheesecake truly special.*

*I make my own lemon marmalade with lemon zest and flesh (discarding the pith), cooking it with sugar and a chopped apple, for more pectin.*

INGREDIENTS
*Serves 4*

- 200g (7oz) Italian breakfast biscuits (Campagnole, or other rustic shortbread biscuits)
- 150g (⅔ cup) butter
- 10g (¼oz) gelatine leaves
- 500g (2 cups) cream cheese
- 120g (1 cup) icing (powdered) sugar
- 1 tablespoon vanilla extract, or the seeds scraped from 1 vanilla pod
- 200ml (¾ cup) double (heavy) cream
- lemon marmalade (shop-bought or homemade, see introduction above)

Blitz the biscuits in a food processor, or place them in a plastic bag and crush with a rolling pin, until you have fine crumbs. Melt the butter gently in a small saucepan or in the microwave. Combine with the biscuit crumbs until evenly mixed.

Line the base of a 22cm (9-inch) springform cake tin with baking paper. Spread the biscuit mixture in the tin and press it firmly with the back of a spoon to create a compact base. Refrigerate for at least 30 minutes.

Soak the gelatine leaves in a small bowl of cold water for about 10 minutes to soften.

In a large bowl, mix the cream cheese with the icing sugar and vanilla extract or seeds until smooth.

In a small pan, heat 3 tablespoons of the cream without boiling. Drain the softened gelatine, squeezing out excess water, and dissolve it in the warm cream, stirring well. Fold this into the cream cheese mixture, stirring thoroughly to avoid lumps.

Whip the remaining cream until stiff peaks form. Gently fold into the cream cheese mixture, using upward motions to keep it airy.

Pour the filling on to the chilled biscuit base, smoothing the surface with a spatula. Cover with clingfilm and refrigerate for at least 4 hours, ideally overnight.

Before serving, remove from the tin and transfer to a serving plate, then spread with a generous layer of lemon marmalade, or serve the plain cheesecake with spoonfuls of the marmalade, if you prefer.

# PUMPKIN PIE

*I spent my first Thanksgiving in New York at the house of a young architect called Nathan, a friend of my American girlfriend Jacqueline, who had invited us as part of a group of friends. The evening was a fascinating introduction to this American tradition, with a gigantic roast turkey and a spiced pumpkin pie with its warm aroma of cinnamon, a dessert completely new to me. That dinner not only introduced me to novel flavours, but has become one of my fondest memories from my youth in New York, a period filled with discovery and unforgettable encounters.*

**INGREDIENTS**
*Serves 4*

- 750g (1lb 10oz) peeled, deseeded and chopped pumpkin or butternut squash
- 350g (12oz) sweet shortcrust pastry
- plain flour, for dusting
- 140g (¾ cup) granulated sugar
- ½ teaspoon salt
- ½ teaspoon freshly grated nutmeg
- 1 teaspoon ground cinnamon
- 2 eggs, lightly beaten
- 25g (2 tablespoons) butter, melted
- 175ml (¾ cup) milk
- 1 tablespoon icing (powdered) sugar

Place the pumpkin in a large saucepan, cover with water and bring to the boil. Cover and simmer for 15 minutes, or until tender. Drain and allow to cool.

Roll out the shortcrust pastry on a lightly floured surface and use it to line a 22cm (9-inch) tart tin. Chill in the refrigerator for 15 minutes.

Preheat the oven to 180°C (350°F), Gas Mark 4.

Line the pastry with baking paper and fill with baking beans to weigh it down. Bake for 15 minutes, then remove the beans and paper and bake for another 10 minutes, until the base is golden and crisp. Remove from the oven and cool slightly.

Increase the oven temperature to 220°C (425°F), Gas Mark 7.

Mash the cooled pumpkin and pass it through a sieve, or blend in a food processor until smooth.

In a bowl, combine the sugar, salt, nutmeg and half the cinnamon. Stir in the beaten eggs, melted butter and milk, then add the mixture to the pumpkin purée. Stir until smooth, then pour into the pastry case. Bake for 10 minutes, then reduce the oven temperature to 180°C (350°F), Gas Mark 4. Continue baking for 35–40 minutes, until the filling is just set.

Let the pie cool before removing from the tin, then chill. Mix the remaining cinnamon with the icing sugar and dust over the top to serve.

# APPLE CAKE

*The aroma of this cake instantly evokes memories of home, family and comfort. It's no coincidence that seasoned American real estate agents often put an apple pie in the oven when showing a house to potential buyers. The simple yet powerful fragrance immediately creates a sense of belonging and warmth. I remember reading a novel in which a character on his deathbed recalled his grandmother's apple cake. Every time I bake this, I can't help but think of that passage and of how deeply food can shape our memories and emotions.*

**INGREDIENTS**
*Serves 4*

- 100ml (scant ½ cup) vegetable oil or melted butter, plus extra (optional) for the tin
- 200g (1¼ cups) plain flour, plus extra (optional) for the tin
- 3 apples, preferably Golden Delicious or Russet (Reinette)
- 3 eggs
- 200g (1 cup) caster (superfine) sugar
- finely grated zest of 1 lemon
- pinch of salt
- 1 tablespoon baking powder
- icing (powdered) sugar, for dusting (optional)

Grease and flour a round cake tin, 24–26cm (9½–10 inches) in diameter, or line the bottom and sides with baking paper. Preheat the oven to 180°C (350°F), Gas Mark 4.

Peel the apples, core them and slice thinly. Set aside.

In a large bowl, whisk the eggs with the sugar until pale and fluffy. Add the lemon zest and salt. Slowly pour in the oil or melted butter while continuing to whisk.

Sift the flour together with the baking powder and fold it gradually into the mixture, stirring gently with a spatula or wooden spoon until smooth.

Fold in half the apple slices, stirring gently to distribute them evenly through the batter.

Pour the batter and apple mixture into the prepared tin. Arrange the remaining apple slices on top in a circle, or any pattern you like. Bake for 40–50 minutes, until golden on top and a skewer inserted into the centre comes out clean.

Leave the cake to cool in the tin for about 10 minutes, then turn out and transfer to a wire rack to cool completely. If desired, dust the top with icing sugar before serving.

## THE EMBRACE *of Light*

On the coldest days, when the world yields to the half-light of winter, our home becomes a haven of warmth and comfort. One of the key elements in creating this enveloping ambience is lighting.

For centuries, during long winters, our ancestors spent their evenings by candlelight. That gentle glow created an intimate atmosphere in which shadows danced across the walls and each flame was a small sanctuary. Of course, there are always exceptions; a game of Scrabble calls for a bright light, while a festive dinner is perfectly lit by a grand chandelier, but the quality of the light remains essential.

My passion for lampshades goes beyond their practical use. Each is a small work of art that adds character to a room. I choose them carefully, favouring fine fabrics and tonal colours that diffuse the light in a soft, flattering way. When I turn on a lamp with a well-chosen shade, a room transforms and the light dances through the fabric, creating its own kind of magic.

Choosing warm light is not only about aesthetics, but also wellbeing. Cool light – which is incredibly valuable in work environments, such as offices and studios – can feel harsh and intrusive at home, while warm, embracing light makes us feel safe and at ease. It is perfect for our homes because it welcomes us and invites us to savour the present moment.

I remember my first trip to Amsterdam and the contrast that struck me between the cool winter light over the canals and the warm glow spilling from the tall windows of houses along the streets. Large lamps, often placed right by the windows, radiated a sense of comfort, making me imagine dinners with friends and family gatherings within.

With these elements in mind, we can create atmospheres that allow us to embrace winter with joy and gratitude. Lamps placed on windowsills, or floor-standing lamps visible from the street, create a welcoming effect even for passers-by outside.

For me, it is essential to reflect on how lighting can be used to recreate the cosy atmosphere of candlelight. Warm light in golden or amber tones brings us closer to that ancient sense of wellbeing. It is a return to our roots, an embracing of tradition, where light does more than illuminate space… it illuminates the soul.

Today, in an age of electricity and abundant lighting, we live in brighter environments, extending our hours of activity beyond the sun's natural rhythm. Yet abundance of light does not always mean comfort. Too often we forget how harsh lighting can affect our spaces, stripping them of warmth.

I particularly love softly lit corners, and I believe that – even in a modern world – there is room for the type of warm, enveloping light that comforted our ancestors. A light that not only brightens, but welcomes and warms.

In the Danish concept of *hygge* – the art of finding happiness in life's simplest pleasures – lighting is a crucial element in creating a sense of cosiness, contentment and wellbeing. When it comes to lighting a room, for me it is essential to choose warm, diffused light. I like to call these lamps 'wells of light': true refuges of warmth. In these corners, a comfortable armchair and a small table lamp become a welcoming nest where I can read, meditate or simply rest.

As a director, I can say that the play between light and shadow renders contours more romantic. On set, when I compose a frame with the director of photography, together we search for the best way in which light can serve the emotional moment of the characters. The atmosphere we create has the power to slow us down, just as nature suggests to us with the arrival of the winter light.

# SPRING

*Nature awakens; the air is alive with scents and blooms. The bees in the garden begin their vital dance.*

As March approaches, the land around our farmhouse starts to come to life once more. The tall mimosas behind the house announce the imminent arrival of spring with their golden plumes. On Mount Costacce, in the forest that has lain bare all winter, white clouds suddenly appear: wild cherry trees adorned with thousands of blossoms. Even though pines, cypresses and Lebanese cedars lend their deep green to the landscape throughout the winter months, the tender green of spring's new shoots always surprises us. Day after day, the scenery grows more vivid, more vibrant. Every corner of the farmhouse is animated with spring colours and scents.

*In spring, birds return from warmer lands; the air fills with their song as they busily set about building their nests.*

The birds return from warmer climates and the air fills with a thousand twitters as they busily build their nests. Hares and squirrels dart among the fresh greenery, while deer with curious eyes and graceful movements bring their young into our woods. Perhaps the mothers choose this place because they feel safe there. We keep the grass cut in the apiary so that we can tend to the bees, creating a clearing around the hives where the fawns roam under the watchful eyes of their mothers. Families of wild boar often cross the land too, rooting about, a vision that feels at once untamed and familiar.

Every nook of the farmhouse's roof offers a refuge for birds; year after year, a robin builds its nest under the pergola where I often sit to work. Even now, as I write, I can hear the flutter of wings and the high-pitched chirrups as it searches for food for its brood. When the fledglings begin to fly, I hang a basket filled with soft cloths beneath the nest, ready to cushion the falls of these young aviators. Each morning, I check the basket and, if need be, place the little ones back in the nest, knowing that the next day they will try again with greater confidence.

With the arrival of spring, daily walks become part of our rhythm once again. A mule track runs alongside the farmhouse before climbing up into the woods, winding around a couple of hairpin bends to a clearing with a few houses and olive groves. From there, the road fades into a narrow path swallowed by vegetation. These hillsides, once planted with chestnut and oak trees by woodsmen of centuries past, have since grown wild. The proximity of the sea has favoured the spread of wild pines, as well as heather, which at this time of year explodes with tiny fragrant blossoms that the bees love, marking the start of their harvesting season.

On these walks, every step reveals new details of the world around us. The resin of the pines and the sweet aroma of the heather mingle with the damp scent of the earth. Sunlight filters through the canopy, casting shifting shadows that dance across the path, turning each footfall into something close to meditation.

In these moments, our dachshunds become indispensable companions. They run ahead, chasing one another, tails wagging with joy. Their sense of wonder at everything they encounter is contagious. Furio and Borlotto, brimming with energy, dash curiously through the undergrowth. Gastone, more cautious, pauses at every new scent. Camillo, the most obedient, walks quietly by my side, observing intently. To the casual eye, it may seem that I am taking them for a walk in the woods, but in truth it's the opposite: they are leading me into another dimension, an inner world, carrying me along a secret passage hidden within the jungle of my own thoughts.

This makes me reflect on dogs in general, because they simply *are*. Here. Now. If a butterfly passes, 'How wonderful!' They chase it. Then suddenly they stop. 'What is that smell? Did you hear that rustle? Let's go and see!' Alessandro says they are like angels because they embody an intrinsic joy in simply being themselves. They choose happiness in the moment, free from complications or thoughts of what might come next.

In the silence of the woods, walking with the dogs, our minds empty. Deep contemplation takes over, listening for that subtle hum, the vibration of the Earth beneath everything else. In this quiet, new ideas emerge… or their absence is allowed. It becomes a time of connection with our deepest selves, that part of us we so often ignore. In this stillness, we begin to understand who we truly are, without masks or preconceptions.

Walking among the trees is more than physical activity. It is a sensory and emotional experience, an immersion into a world pulsating with life and beauty. It is a journey of discovery, an invitation to witness the awakening of nature, to appreciate its simplicity and its magnificence. I end each springtime walk with a lighter heart and a renewed spirit, grateful for the time spent in pure harmony and grace.

# ACQUA COTTA

*This recipe belongs to that family of humble peasant dishes made from very little: a simple and hearty soup that comforts the soul. Celery, tomatoes, a few other vegetables, fresh herbs, stale bread and an egg in each bowl for substance. It's one of the soups my grandfather mentioned when he spoke about the war. As a child, I spent my summers in Casentino, in Stia, with my father's family. Surrounded by cousins, we often ended up at a small restaurant on the banks of the Arno. Stia is where the Arno, flowing down from Mount Falterona, meets its first tributary, the Staggia, and gains the strength of a true river. Acqua cotta brings me back to those summer days in the woods, those long lunches and plunging into the Arno's icy, crystal-clear waters.*

INGREDIENTS
*Serves 4*

- 2–3 onions, 300–400g (10½–14oz) in total
- 1 head of celery, about 400g (14oz)
- 400g (14oz) can of peeled tomatoes
- handful of basil leaves, about 10g (½ cup) loosely packed
- 4 eggs
- 4 slices of rustic bread, about 200g (7oz) total weight
- extra virgin olive oil
- 50g (½ cup) grated pecorino cheese
- salt and freshly ground black pepper

Roughly chop the onions and slice the celery stalks into rounds, then put them in a saucepan, or an earthenware flameproof casserole dish if you have one. Finely chop the celery leaves and add them as well. Crush the peeled tomatoes by hand before adding them to the dish. Add the basil, salt, pepper and enough water to cover everything. Place over the heat and let simmer for about 1 hour, until the onions become translucent.

Crack the eggs directly into the soup so they poach in the broth; let them cook for about 3 minutes, until the whites are set but the yolks are still creamy. Meanwhile, toast the bread.

When the soup is ready, place a slice of toasted bread drizzled with olive oil in each bowl and sprinkle it with pecorino. Ladle the soup over the bread, making sure each serving gets a poached egg cooked just right, with the yolk soft and velvety.

STAUB
STAUB

# BIANCA'S STEW

*Nothing makes my daughter Bianca happier than a plate of stew: the aroma of the sauce with potatoes, the tender pieces that fall apart after cooking long and slow... I wanted to find a way to recreate those flavours in a vegetarian recipe, and luckily discovered Vis Naturae, a small artisanal workshop that produces seitan with a truly unique taste. Domenico, the owner, is a kind and generous soul who shared with me his recipe for making seitan, which absorbs the aromas of the sauce it cooks in. Every time Bianca comes to visit me, I prepare this dish with pride, knowing I've created something that nourishes not only the body, but also the bond between us.*

INGREDIENTS
*Serves 4*

*For homemade seitan*

- 1.5kg (12 cups) plain flour
- generous dash of tamari
- kombu seaweed

*For the stew*

- 800g (1lb 12oz) potatoes
- 1 red onion
- extra virgin olive oil
- 2 chopped bay leaves or 1 teaspoon ground bay leaves
- pinch of chilli flakes
- 500ml (2 cups) tomato passata
- 1 teaspoon tomato purée (optional)
- salt and freshly ground black pepper

You can buy seitan in most health food stores (you will need 900g/2lb for this recipe), but if you have time, you can make it yourself. To do so, knead the flour with just enough water to make a dough for about 30 minutes. Rinse the dough in a bowl of water a couple of times to remove the starch, which makes it softer and silkier, then shape into a ball. Bring a saucepan of water to the boil. Add the seitan and return to the boil, then drain and slice about 2.5cm (1 inch) thick. Bring a saucepan of fresh water to the boil with the tamari and kombu. Add your sliced seitan to the flavoured water and simmer for 40–45 minutes, then leave to cool.

For the stew, wash and peel the potatoes (you can soak the peels in water to make snacks later, see page 25). Cut them into large chunks and set aside. Roughly chop the onion.

Place a cast-iron casserole dish, which is perfect for cooking slowly, over a medium heat. Pour in enough olive oil to cover the bottom of the dish and add the onion. When it begins to sizzle, stir in the bay leaves. Once the onion becomes translucent, after about 5 minutes, add the potatoes, chilli flakes and salt. Cover with a lid and cook gently over a low heat.

After about 5 minutes, stir in the passata and enough water to almost cover the potatoes. Cook gently for at least 30 minutes, stirring occasionally and adjusting the seasoning.

Meanwhile, cut the seitan into large cubes and sauté it in olive oil in a wok or nonstick pan, browning all sides until they form a darker crust. Remove from the heat.

When the potatoes are tender and the sauce has thickened, add the tomato purée, if using. Push the potatoes to one side of the pan, add the sautéed seitan and stir well so it absorbs the rich sauce.

Serve with a drizzle of olive oil and a twist of black pepper.

# COBB SALAD FOR OLIVIA

*I've shared many experiences with my friend Olivia, a Roman woman of great temperament and character. We were business partners for a while, and always remained close, even when our ventures didn't go as planned. Olivia loves food and has a unique gift for transforming even the simplest dish into something extraordinary. When she cooks, she starts with one idea and ends up somewhere completely different, boldly adding ingredients along the way. The result is always exceptional and that's why I dedicate this Cobb salad to her.*

INGREDIENTS
*Serves 4*

- 2–3 slices of stale bread, about 100g (3½oz), cut into cubes
- 3–4 tablespoons extra virgin olive oil
- 4 eggs
- 1 head of radicchio, about 250g (9oz)
- 1 Iceberg lettuce, about 400g (14oz)
- 2 apples, about 300g (10½oz) total weight
- 1 mozzarella ball, ideally fior di latte, about 125g (4½oz)
- 40g (scant ½ cup) grated Parmesan cheese, or to taste
- 30g (¼ cup) raisins
- 40g (¼ cup) cashew nuts or walnuts
- salt
- daisies, to serve (optional)

*For the vinaigrette*

- 4 tablespoons extra virgin olive oil
- 2 tablespoons apple cider vinegar
- 1 garlic clove
- freshly ground black pepper

Preheat the oven to 180°C (350°F), Gas Mark 4.

Arrange the bread cubes in a nonstick baking tray, brush with some of the olive oil and season with salt. In another small, well-oiled tray, crack the eggs so they spread out evenly, then add a pinch of salt. Place both trays in the oven.

When the bread is golden and the eggs are set (the whites should be dry), remove the trays and let them cool.

Wash and finely chop the radicchio and lettuce, then put them in a salad bowl. Wash, peel and finely dice the apples and finely dice the mozzarella. Add the chopped apple and both cheeses to the salad bowl with the raisins and nuts.

To make the vinaigrette, whisk the olive oil and apple cider vinegar together in a separate bowl. Smash the garlic clove with the side of a blade, add it to the bowl and leave to infuse for about 10 minutes. Remove the garlic and season the vinaigrette with salt and pepper.

Cut the eggs into small cubes and add them to the salad bowl. About 15 minutes before serving, add the croutons and toss everything in the vinaigrette. Scatter with daisies, if you like, to serve.

# SALAD WITH TAHINI

*My friend Phyllis was more than just a manager to me; she was an inspiration. Originally from Chicago, but of Lebanese heritage, Phyllis had worked in Hollywood alongside some of the biggest names in cinema. Her stories were fascinating, a bridge linking to the industry's old glamour. One of the recipes she loved to share was this salad. Every time I make it, I am transported back to the hills of Los Angeles, where Phyllis and I would sit sipping rosé and dreaming of the future. It's more than just a salad to me; it's a vivid memory of a friendship that made a deep impression on my life. The method below is for a traditional chopped salad, but I sometimes make a version using a whole romaine lettuce heart, as in the photo.*

INGREDIENTS
*Serves 4*

- 800g (1lb 12oz) sweet potatoes
- 4 tablespoons extra virgin olive oil
- 2 teaspoons dried thyme
- 2 teaspoons cumin seeds
- 2 garlic cloves, crushed
- 800g (5½ cups) chickpeas (garbanzo beans), home-cooked or jarred, drained
- 2 tablespoons lemon juice
- 200ml (¾ cup) boiling water
- 4 tablespoons tahini
- 4 large romaine lettuce leaves, chopped
- bunch of parsley, about 50g (1¾oz), chopped
- 4 tablespoons pumpkin seeds (optional)
- 100g (⅔ cup) crumbled feta cheese (optional)
- salt and freshly ground black pepper

Preheat the oven to 200°C (400°F), Gas Mark 6.

Peel the sweet potatoes and cut them into 4cm (1½-inch) chunks. Place them in a large baking tray, season with half the olive oil, thyme, ½ teaspoon of salt and ½ teaspoon of black pepper. Toss well so the chunks are evenly coated, then roast for 20 minutes, until tender. Leave to cool in the tray.

In a dry pan, toast the cumin seeds over a medium heat until fragrant, then crush them in a mortar. Warm the remaining olive oil in a saucepan, add the cumin and garlic and sauté gently for 1 minute.

Add the chickpeas, lemon juice, measured boiling water, 1 teaspoon of salt and ½ teaspoon of black pepper. Reduce the heat, cover and cook for 10–15 minutes, until the chickpeas are soft. Remove the lid and cook for a few more minutes to let any remaining liquid evaporate. Set aside to cool.

Prepare the tahini sauce: in a small bowl, combine the tahini and ¼ teaspoon each of salt and black pepper. Stir with a fork, adjusting the seasoning and adding a little water if needed to achieve the consistency of runny honey.

To assemble, place the chopped lettuce, parsley, chickpeas and sweet potatoes in a large serving bowl. Drizzle with the tahini sauce and toss well. Finish with the pumpkin seeds, crumbled feta and a generous twist of black pepper.

Alternatively, if you want to recreate the presentation in the photo, wash a romaine lettuce heart by immersing it upside down in cold water. Drain thoroughly, then carefully trim off the base so that the leaves remain attached but open up slightly.

Place the tahini sauce in a large bowl, then rotate the lettuce heart in the dressing, so the leaves are coated from the inside out. Invert the lettuce onto a plate and scatter the remaining ingredients over the top.

STAUB

# GORGONZOLA MILLEFOGLIE

*My Aunt Patrizia, once my maths teacher and now retired, never sits still. Between her volunteer work and her role as a grandmother, she always finds time to discover new recipes to delight us with whenever the family gathers at her house. I lost both my parents at a very young age and it was she, my mother's sister, who stepped in to help raise us; she has the gift of bringing everyone together with her warm spirit and her passion for cooking. Aunt Patrizia once surprised us with this millefoglie, where the creaminess of Gorgonzola meets the sweetness of apple and the crunch of walnuts. It is finished with a drizzle of acacia honey; ours comes from the hives at Le Gusciane, making the dish feel even more like home.*

INGREDIENTS
*Serves 4*

- butter, for the dish
- 270g (9¾oz) packet of filo pastry
- 1 Golden Delicious apple
- 200g (7oz) Gorgonzola cheese
- 2 eggs
- 150g (⅔ cup) single (light) cream
- 50g (¼ cup plus 1 tablespoon) walnut halves
- rosemary leaves
- 1 tablespoon acacia honey
- salt and freshly ground black pepper

Butter a baking dish and preheat the oven to 180°C (350°F), Gas Mark 4.

Crumple the filo sheets one by one into pleats and arrange them side by side in the dish until they resemble an accordion.

Wash the apple, cut it in half, remove the core, and slice into 3mm (⅛-inch) wedges. Insert the apple slices between the folds of the pastry. Do the same with thin slices of Gorgonzola, tucking them in carefully without pressing too much.

In a large bowl, beat the eggs with the cream and a pinch each of salt and pepper. Pour the mixture into the dish, making sure it seeps between the folds without drowning them. Break the walnut halves into pieces, scatter them over along with the rosemary leaves, then bake for 40 minutes.

Once out of the oven, let the millefoglie rest for 5 minutes, then drizzle lightly and evenly with the acacia honey before serving.

# LENTIL, BEETROOT, FETA AND AVOCADO SALAD

*One evening while preparing dinner, I realized I had accidentally mixed up two different menus. I rushed to fix my mistake, of course, but ended up with lots of leftover ingredients and no idea what to do with them. Fortunately, my friend Benedetta was with me. With her expert eye, she took those ingredients and composed a salad. After service, we sat down at the table and enjoyed that improvised creation. It was the perfect conclusion to a rather hectic evening… and proof that sometimes the best recipes are born by chance.*

*For a finishing touch, you can add fresh herbs, such as parsley or coriander, or for extra crunch, toasted nuts or seeds.*

INGREDIENTS
*Serves 4*

- 200g (1 cup) large green lentils
- 1 litre (4 cups) vegetable stock (broth)
- 2 beetroot (beets)
- extra virgin olive oil
- 2 ripe avocados
- 150g (5½oz) feta cheese
- salt and freshly ground black pepper

*For the vinaigrette*

- 2 tablespoons lime juice
- 4 tablespoons extra virgin olive oil

Rinse the lentils under cold running water. Meanwhile, bring the vegetable stock to the boil in a large saucepan. Add the lentils and cook over a medium heat for 25–30 minutes, until tender but still holding their shape. Drain and allow to cool.

Wash the beetroot thoroughly and boil in a pan of salted water for 40–50 minutes, until tender. Drain, cool and peel.

Preheat the oven to 180°C (350°F), Gas Mark 4. Cut the beetroot into cubes and season with olive oil, salt and pepper. Place in a baking tray lined with baking paper and roast for about 15 minutes, until slightly crisp.

Peel the avocados and cut them into slices or cubes, as you prefer.

For the vinaigrette, whisk together the lime juice and olive oil in a small bowl. Season with salt and pepper.

In a large serving bowl, gently combine the cooled lentils with the roasted beetroot. Add the avocados and crumble in the feta, then drizzle with the lime vinaigrette and toss carefully. Alternatively, make a base of the lentils and arrange the other ingredients on top. Serve on individual plates, or on a large platter.

# AEGINA HALLOUMI SALAD

*Two years ago, on Aegina, a small Greek island near Athens, I had the opportunity to work on a film with my daughter Bianca. Every evening after shooting, we explored the local tavernas. It was in one of those little restaurants that we discovered this salad. Bianca, a great lover of cheese, instantly fell in love with the dish, and her enthusiasm made those dinners even more special.*

INGREDIENTS
*Serves 4*

- 3 sweet potatoes, about 1.2kg (2lb 12oz) total weight
- extra virgin olive oil
- 2 tablespoons apple cider vinegar
- finely grated zest of 1 lemon
- 2 handfuls of rocket
- 180g (6oz) cherry tomatoes
- 1 ripe avocado
- small handful of mint leaves
- small handful of basil leaves
- 250g (9oz) halloumi cheese
- salt and freshly ground black pepper

Preheat the oven to 200°C (400°F), Gas Mark 6.

Peel the sweet potatoes and cut them into wedges. Place them in a baking tray, drizzle with 2 tablespoons of olive oil, season with salt and pepper and roast for about 30 minutes, until tender but still holding their shape.

Make the dressing by mixing 4 tablespoons of olive oil with the apple cider vinegar, lemon zest and salt and pepper in a bowl.

Once cooled, transfer the sweet potatoes to a salad bowl and add the rocket and cherry tomatoes. Slice the avocado and chop the herbs, add both to the bowl, then toss well with the dressing.

Warm a little olive oil in a frying pan, add the halloumi and sear on both sides until golden. Arrange the cheese over the salad and serve.

# AVOCADO TOAST

*I first ate avocado toast in a small restaurant on Melrose, in Beverly Hills, and instantly fell in love. Years later, while working on a film set in England, I had a production assistant who brought a slice to my trailer every day as a snack. I remember thinking, 'I have an assistant making me avocado toast: I've made it!' I have now learned how to make it myself. The acidity of the lime juice and the soft yolk of the poached egg make this dish both delicious and balanced: the healthy fats in the avocado, the protein in the egg and the carbohydrates in the bread are the perfect way to start the day. And nowadays, you can even find avocados grown in Sicily.*

INGREDIENTS
*Serves 4*

- 1 tablespoon apple cider vinegar
- 4 eggs
- 2 ripe avocados
- juice of 1 lime
- extra virgin olive oil
- bread
- chilli flakes
- sea salt flakes

Bring a small saucepan of water to the boil with the vinegar and a pinch of salt. Crack one egg at a time into a small sieve to remove the thinner part of the white. Reduce the heat under the saucepan, swirl the water to create a vortex, then gently drop in the egg. Poach for about 2 minutes, until the white is set but the yolk is still soft. Remove with a slotted spoon and repeat with the remaining eggs.

Halve the avocados, remove the stones and scoop the flesh into a small bowl. Mash with a fork or potato masher until creamy, then stir in the lime juice, a little olive oil and a pinch of salt.

Slice the bread about 1.5cm (½ inch) thick and toast until golden. Drizzle with olive oil and sprinkle with salt. Spread the avocado mixture over the toast, top with a poached egg, then finish with a drizzle of olive oil and a dusting of chilli flakes. Your toast is ready!

# FILO STICKS WITH FETA, ASPARAGUS AND SPINACH

*I'm always looking for new ideas to serve at our farmhouse aperitivi because I tend to get a little bored with the usual hummus, farinata and potato skins. One day, while browsing online for inspiration, I came across vegetable-filled filo sticks. They're a charming idea and allow me to experiment with different fillings, such as asparagus or sautéed spinach.*

INGREDIENTS
*Serves 4*

- 1 small onion
- 2 garlic cloves
- extra virgin olive oil
- 200g (7oz) fresh spinach
- 6 tablespoons crumbled feta cheese
- 12 sheets of filo pastry
- 4 tablespoons melted butter
- 1 tablespoon chopped mint leaves, plus a few leaves to serve
- 6 asparagus tips, trimmed
- 1 tablespoon black sesame seeds
- honey
- salt and freshly ground black pepper

Finely chop the onion and garlic. In a pan, warm a little olive oil and sauté the onion and garlic until golden. Add the spinach and cook for a few minutes, until wilted. Remove from the heat and allow to cool. Mix in half the feta and season with salt and pepper.

Brush 1 sheet of filo with melted butter, lay another sheet on top, and brush with butter again. Cut the double sheet in half widthways (keep the remaining filo covered with a damp cloth so it doesn't dry out).

Preheat the oven to 180°C (350°F), Gas Mark 4.

For the asparagus sticks: place some of the remaining crumbled feta, the chopped mint, and an asparagus tip on the lower half of the filo sheet. Roll tightly to form a stick, tucking in the ends, then brush with melted butter and sprinkle with black sesame seeds. Make 5 more sticks in the same way.

For the spinach sticks, place a spoonful of the spinach mixture on the lower half of the prepared filo sheet. Roll tightly to form a stick, tucking in the ends, thenbrush with melted butter and sprinkle with black sesame seeds. Make 5 more sticks in the same way.

Arrange the sticks in a baking tray lined with baking paper. Bake until golden; this should take about 20 minutes, but keep an eye on them so they don't catch.

Once baked, drizzle lightly with honey, scatter with mint leaves and cool to room temperature before serving.

# SANGEETA'S CURRY

*Curry only entered my life after I turned forty, thanks to my friend Sangeeta, a London-based interior designer with an extraordinary talent for cooking. The dinners at her home are among my fondest memories of the years I spent living in London. We shared many culinary exchanges: I taught her my secret pizza recipe, while she opened the door for me to the magic of curry.*

INGREDIENTS
*Serves 4*

- 1 cauliflower
- 400g (14oz) can of butter beans, drained
- 1 tablespoon Thai red or green curry paste
- 400g (14oz) can of coconut milk
- 300g (1½ cups) basmati rice
- large handful of fresh spinach
- salt

Wash the cauliflower and cut it into florets. Place them in a large saucepan along with the butter beans, curry paste and coconut milk. Cover with a lid and cook gently over a low heat for 15 minutes, or until the cauliflower is tender but not falling apart.

Meanwhile, cook the basmati rice in a separate saucepan according to the packet instructions. Generally, for 1½ cups of rice, use 3 cups of water and a pinch of salt. The rice is ready when it has fully absorbed the water.

When the cauliflower is almost cooked, take off the heat, add the spinach, cover, and leave for 5 minutes so the spinach wilts. Stir well, adjust the seasoning if needed and serve alongside the rice.

# SAVOURY KEY LIME PIE

*Another recipe inspired by desserts! Key lime pie is a speciality from Key West, at the southern tip of Florida. I first tasted the classic sweet version in Miami, at a New Year's Eve celebration at the turn of the millennium. It didn't quite win me over, but its bright citrus twist fascinated me and the look of the pie stayed in my mind. That's how this savoury cheesecake was born, a dish that recalls Caribbean holidays, where the scent of the lime in mojitos mingles with mint and cane sugar.*

INGREDIENTS
*Serves 4*

- 250g (9oz) stale bread
- extra virgin olive oil
- 2 ripe avocados
- juice of 1 lime
- 100g (3½oz) mozzarella ball, ideally fior di latte
- 100g (½ cup) cottage cheese, drained
- 1 burrata cheese, about 150g (5½oz)
- salt and freshly ground black pepper

*For the vinaigrette*

- 40g (2 cups loosely packed) basil leaves
- 10g (½ cup loosely packed) mint leaves, plus extra to serve
- 4 tablespoons extra virgin olive oil
- 2 tablespoons apple cider vinegar
- juice of 1 lime
- 1 teaspoon honey

Preheat the oven to 180°C (350°F), Gas Mark 4.

For the vinaigrette, combine all the ingredients in a blender. Blend until smooth, then adjust the seasoning with salt.

Cut the bread into cubes, toss with olive oil and salt and toast in the oven for 10 minutes, or until golden.

Halve the avocados, remove the stones, scoop the flesh into a bowl and mash with a fork. Season with the lime juice, a little olive oil, salt and pepper.

Tear the mozzarella into pieces and mix with the drained cottage cheese in a bowl. Tear in the burrata and combine well.

When ready to serve, assemble individual pies directly on the plates using a pastry ring. Start with a small spoonful of the cheese mixture at the bottom, to keep the base from sliding. Add a layer of toasted croutons, then a thick layer of the cheese mixture. Spoon a little vinaigrette over the cheese, then cover with a layer of mashed avocado.

Finish with a drizzle of olive oil, some mint leaves and a twist of fresh black pepper.

STAUB

# DARSENA LASAGNE

*Valeria is a true force of nature in the kitchen. Her cooking at the Bagno Arizona beach club has become a point of reference for the whole Darsena (harbour) of Viareggio, a coastal region near Lucca. She's always searching for new ideas to bring to the table. Sometimes she lets me peek into her notebook, a treasure trove of recipes collected over time. One of her most exquisite creations is this vegetarian lasagne, which she generously shared with me. Every bite is a delight, and I am truly grateful to include her wonderful recipe in this book.*

INGREDIENTS
*Serves 4*

*For the fresh pasta (optional)*

- 300g (2½ cups) '00' flour
- 3 eggs
- pinch of salt

*For the vegetables*

- 2 fennel bulbs, about 400g (14oz)
- 2 carrots, about 200g (7oz)
- 2 courgettes (zucchini), about 250g (9oz)
- extra virgin olive oil
- 2 shallots, about 60g (2¼oz), finely chopped
- salt and freshly ground black pepper

*For the whipped butter*

- 100g (7 tbsp) softened butter
- 50ml (¼ cup) sparkling water

*For the besciamella*

- 1 litre (4 cups) whole milk
- 100g (¾ cup) plain flour
- nutmeg

*To assemble the lasagne*

- lasagne sheets, homemade or dried
- 300g (10½oz) smoked buffalo scamorza cheese, sliced
- thyme leaves (optional)

If you want to make the fresh pasta, place the flour in a mound on a work surface, make a well in the centre and add the eggs and salt. Knead until smooth and elastic. Cover with a tea towel and leave to rest for 30 minutes. Roll out the dough with a rolling pin or pasta machine into very thin sheets. Alternatively, use 12 sheets of dried pasta, cooked according to the packet instructions.

For the vegetables, wash and trim the fennel, carrots and courgettes, then dice them. In a large frying pan, warm a little olive oil and sauté the shallots until translucent. Add the diced vegetables and cook over a medium heat for 10–15 minutes, until tender but still crisp. Season with salt and pepper and set aside.

For the whipped butter, beat the softened butter with the sparkling water until fluffy and set aside.

For the besciamella, warm the milk in a saucepan over a medium heat. In another pan, lightly toast the flour, stirring continuously for a few minutes. Gradually add the hot milk to the flour, whisking to prevent lumps. Cook until slightly thickened. Add salt and grated nutmeg, to taste. Remove from the heat and gently fold in the whipped butter, stirring until smooth and slightly loose.

Preheat the oven to 180°C (350°F), Gas Mark 4.

In a baking dish, spread a thin layer of besciamella, then cover with sheets of pasta. Spread with some of the sautéed vegetables, another layer of besciamella, and a few slices of smoked buffalo scamorza. Continue layering like this until all the ingredients are used up, finishing with a layer of pasta topped with besciamella and scamorza slices.

Cover the dish with foil and bake for 35–40 minutes. Remove the foil and bake for another 10–15 minutes, until golden and crisp, then serve scattered with thyme leaves, if you like.

# RICOTTA AND SPINACH RAVIOLI

*This is a true Italian classic, but as a boy, I didn't really love ravioli; I only began to enjoy it properly once I arrived in Camaiore and met Tatiana. Tatiana is boisterous, fun and a wonderful cook, and I immediately fell for her ravioli: large, rustic, made with a rough-textured dough and a truly bulging pillow of filling, they are as generous as Tatiana is with the time she so kindly shares with me. Every time she invents a new recipe, she calls and says, 'Calvani, come over, let's try another one!'*

**INGREDIENTS**
*Serves 4*

*For the pasta*

- 850g (6½ cups) plain flour
- 150g (1 cup) semolina
- 5 eggs
- 1 tablespoon extra virgin olive oil
- 100ml (½ cup) whole milk
- salt

*For the filling*

- 2kg (4lb 8oz) spinach
- 500g (1lb 2oz) sheep's milk ricotta cheese
- 4 eggs
- 150g (1½ cups) grated Parmesan cheese
- nutmeg

*To serve*

- butter
- sage leaves
- toasted cashew nuts, chopped
- shaved Parmesan or pecorino cheese

Form a mound with the flour and combine with most of the semolina, keeping a small handful aside for dusting. Make a well in the centre. Add the eggs, olive oil, milk and a pinch of salt. Work quickly with your fingers until you form a firm dough (a stand mixer is faster, but I recommend finishing with a few kneads by hand). Wrap the dough in a tea towel and let it rest in the refrigerator for 1 hour.

Wash the spinach, place in a saucepan and cook for a few minutes, until wilted. Remove from the heat and allow to cool, then squeeze the leaves very well to press out any remaining water. You should have 1kg (2lb 4oz) of cooked spinach. Chop it coarsely, ideally with a mezzaluna (be careful not to chop too finely, or the mixture will lose that rustic texture). Squeeze again after chopping. In a bowl, stir the spinach with the ricotta, eggs, Parmesan, a grating of nutmeg and a pinch of salt.

After it has rested, roll out the dough with a rolling pin until it's about 1mm (1/32 inch) thick, or use a pasta machine to reach the same thickness. Using a piping bag, place small mounds of filling about 5cm (2 inches) apart on the dough. Fold the sheet over, press down around each mound of filling to remove the air, then cut into squares with a pastry wheel.

Cook the ravioli in a saucepan in plenty of salted boiling water until they rise to the surface. Meanwhile, melt the butter in a frying pan and add the sage leaves. Drain the ravioli and serve with the butter and sage, finishing with toasted, chopped cashews for a crunchy touch. Finally, sprinkle with the Parmesan or pecorino shavings.

# FLORENTINE RISOTTO

*Luisa is an elegant, cultured woman, but that doesn't stop her from telling you exactly what's on her mind. In that sense, she perfectly embodies the Florentine spirit: those born in the shadow of Giotto's bell tower never hold back with their opinions. I've always wondered how Florentines manage to live surrounded by so much beauty; Florence never ceases to amaze, with its architectural and artistic masterpieces around every corner. Whenever I meet Luisa, we go for lunch at one of the city's historic trattorias, and at some point in the conversation, we always end up talking about recipes such as this, which she kindly shared with me.*

INGREDIENTS
*Serves 4*

- 1 litre (4 cups) vegetable stock (broth)
- extra virgin olive oil
- 30g (2 tablespoons) butter
- 1 small onion, chopped
- 400g (2 cups) risotto rice, such as arborio or carnaroli
- 100ml (½ cup) dry white wine
- 200g (7oz) fresh spinach
- 150g (⅔ cup) mascarpone cheese
- 100g (1 cup) grated Parmesan cheese
- 30g (¼ cup) unsalted pistachios
- 80g (3oz) stracciatella cheese
- salt and freshly ground black pepper

Prepare the stock and keep it warm over a low heat while making the risotto.

In a wide pan, warm a drizzle of olive oil with half the butter. Add the chopped onion and sauté until translucent.

Add the rice and toast for a couple of minutes, stirring constantly, until slightly translucent. Pour in the white wine and let the alcohol evaporate over a high heat, stirring continuously.

Begin adding the hot stock a ladleful at a time, waiting until it is almost fully absorbed before adding more. Continue this process for 15–18 minutes, until the rice is al dente.

Meanwhile, wash the spinach and blitz it with the mascarpone in a food processor or with a hand blender until smooth.

When the rice is nearly ready, stir in the spinach-mascarpone cream and the Parmesan. Stir well and cook for another 2–3 minutes, until the risotto is creamy and the spinach is heated through.

Remove from the heat, add the remaining butter and stir vigorously to emulsify. Adjust the seasoning with salt and pepper.

Roughly chop the pistachios. Serve the risotto topped with a spoonful of stracciatella and a sprinkle of pistachios.

# SEITAN STRACCETTI WITH ARTICHOKES

*One of my favourite dishes from the Roman tradition is straccetti with artichokes. When I was working at RAI (Italy's national public broadcasting company), I used to eat it at a trattoria tucked just behind the Teatro delle Vittorie that was well known among TV workers. The place is called Da Dante, and their straccetti con i carciofe was exceptional. I often went there with my agent, Rosaria, and it wasn't unusual to bump into famous Italian TV personalities. Once I moved to Le Gusciane, I felt the urge to create my own version of the dish, with seitan instead of the traditional strips of beef or veal, and the result was truly outstanding. I'm very proud of it.*

*In this dish, the artichokes become very creamy after cooking. You can emphasize this effect if you like, by blitzing half of the braised artichokes to a purée and serving the remaining ones and the sautéed seitan on top.*

INGREDIENTS
*Serves 4*

- 4 artichokes, about 500g (1lb 2oz) total weight
- juice of 1 lemon
- 60ml (¼ cup) extra virgin olive oil
- 2 garlic cloves, crushed
- 200ml (¾ cup) water
- 500g (1lb 2oz) seitan, thinly sliced into strips (for homemade, see page 133)
- 100ml (½ cup) white wine
- about 10g (¼oz) chopped parsley leaves (optional)
- salt and freshly ground black pepper

Clean the artichokes by removing the tough outer leaves, trimming the tops and peeling the stems. Cut them in half, remove the inner chokes, then slice thinly and place in water with a little of the lemon juice added to prevent browning.

In a wide saucepan, warm half the olive oil with 1 crushed garlic clove. Add the drained artichokes, the juice of ½ lemon, the water, salt and pepper. Cover with baking paper and cook over a medium-low heat for 20–25 minutes, until the artichokes are tender.

In another pan, warm the remaining olive oil with the remaining crushed garlic clove. Add the seitan and sauté for a few minutes. Deglaze with the white wine and let the alcohol evaporate. Cook for 5–7 minutes, until the seitan is nicely golden.

Once the artichokes are ready, add them to the seitan. Stir well and let everything cook together for 2–3 minutes. Serve hot, scattered with chopped parsley, if you like.

# SEMOLINA TART

*Simona, my husband Alessandro's sister, is a dedicated baker with a special love for traditional cakes. She's always eager to experiment, but she shines above all in the classics, such as apple pie and this semolina tart, which is her own recipe. Simona began baking this delight for us during our yoga retreats and brunches, and eventually taught me how to make it. So here it is: the Franchini family's semolina tart, a true treasure.*

INGREDIENTS
*Serves 4*

*For the pastry base and lattice*

- 4 eggs
- 200g (1 cup) caster (superfine) sugar
- 160ml (⅔ cup) sunflower oil, plus extra for the tin
- 640g (5 cups) plain flour, plus extra for dusting and for the tin
- 1 teaspoon baking powder
- finely grated zest of ½ lemon

*For the semolina filling*

- 1 litre (4 cups) whole milk
- 150g (1 cup) semolina
- 100g (7 tablespoons) butter
- 100g (½ cup) vanilla sugar, or granulated sugar plus 1 teaspoon vanilla extract
- 200g (1 cup) unflavoured granulated sugar
- 3 egg yolks
- finely grated zest of 1 lemon
- splash of liqueur (we use moscato, vermouth or brandy)

*To serve (optional)*

- icing (powdered) sugar, for dusting
- fruit coulis

For the pastry, beat the eggs with the sugar in a bowl until light and frothy. Add the sunflower oil and stir well. Gradually sift in the flour with the baking powder, stirring until smooth and homogeneous. Stir in the grated lemon zest, wrap the dough in clingfilm and let it rest in the refrigerator for at least 30 minutes.

For the filling, bring the milk to the boil in a saucepan. Gradually pour in the semolina, whisking constantly to avoid lumps. Cook over a medium heat for about 10 minutes, until thick and fully cooked. Remove from the heat and stir in the butter until melted, then add the vanilla sugar and unflavoured granulated sugar, stirring well. Allow the mixture to cool slightly, then add the egg yolks one at a time, stirring after each addition. Finally, add the lemon zest and liqueur.

Preheat the oven to 180°C (350°F), Gas Mark 4.

Roll out the pastry on a floured surface to about 1cm (½ inch) thick.

Now pick your tart tin. With the quantities specified here, I often make 2 × 24cm (9½-inch) tarts, or you can make one large 30cm (12-inch) tart. Oil and flour your chosen tart tin(s), then line them with the pastry, leaving a raised edge. Pour in the semolina filling and smooth with a spatula.

Reroll the remaining pastry, cut into strips and arrange them on top in a lattice pattern. Bake for 40–45 minutes, until golden and the filling is set. Remove from the oven and allow to cool before serving.

This is delicious at room temperature, or slightly warmed. You can serve it with a dusting of icing sugar or a fruit coulis.

# FRIED WISTERIA BLOSSOMS

*In early spring, our pergolas at the farmhouse are covered in cascades of purple wisteria, creating an enchanting and majestic effect. The spectacle has always sparked my culinary curiosity, so I began searching for recipes that could make use of such abundance... and discovered fried wisteria blossoms. The dish is surprising in both its simplicity and captivating taste. I love serving it to our guests and watching their astonishment; it adds a magical touch that makes our time together even more special.*

INGREDIENTS
*Serves 4*

- 15 clusters of wisteria blossoms, 60–80g (2¼–2¾oz) total weight
- about 500ml (2 cups) sunflour oil
- 200ml (¾ cup) water
- about 50g (¼ cup) granulated sugar, to taste
- 150g (1¼ cups) plain flour

After harvesting the wisteria blossoms, shake them gently and check that no leaves or insects remain. Remove the stems: while wisteria flowers are edible and delicious, the stems are not.

Warm the oil in a large, deep pan over a medium-high heat.

In a bowl, combine the measured water and sugar, whisking until the sugar dissolves. Gradually add the flour, stirring continuously until you have a smooth, fluid batter.

To check if the oil is hot enough, dip in the handle of a wooden spoon: if bubbles form around it, the oil is ready for frying.

Dip the wisteria blossoms into the batter, making sure they are well coated, and fry them in the hot oil until golden and crisp.

Place the fried blossoms on a tray lined with kitchen paper to blot off the excess oil. Enjoy once slightly cooled.

When furnishing a home, colour plays a fundamental role, especially in a country setting like ours. Colours not only define a space, but also influence our mood and our perception of the rooms. In a country house, it is important that they evoke serenity and warmth, blending harmoniously with the natural surroundings.

## THE LANGUAGE *of colour*

I believe the hand of an interior designer should be light, almost imperceptible. The goal is for the result to feel so harmonious that it seems natural, with no obvious trace of the designer's presence. This subtlety allows people to feel welcomed and at ease, without the décor becoming intrusive or overwhelming. When I began planning the rooms at Le Gusciane, I carried around a colour chart in my pocket for weeks. I wanted the interiors to relate naturally to the exterior of the farmhouse, creating warm and inviting spaces.

On social media, one often sees bold hues and dramatic contrasts. These effects are striking, but they did not suit my vision. I wanted each room to have its own colour scheme, but without the eye perceiving any abrupt changes as you walk from one to the next. My aim was to create atmosphere, while still embracing white as the backdrop, a canvas to highlight the wooden ceiling beams and the terracotta tiles. I decided to paint the upper portion of the walls white, and then, about ten centimetres (four inches) below the line of the beams, introduce a tone that at first glance also appeared white, but in truth carried a subtle shade, just enough to support the stronger tones of the furniture, panelling and textiles. I often used paintings as inspiration for the colour palette, works I had found in flea markets that moved me.

On the ground floor, I chose shades that would harmonize with the colour of the gravel in the courtyard and the stone walls. The main paint I used is Strong White by Farrow & Ball, a white with sandy undertones that pairs beautifully with the royal blue of the kitchen and the lichen green of the shelves. It creates a warm background that unites everything else, from the olive-green cushions in the entrance to the large wall on which our hand-painted porcelain is displayed with our collection of gin. To guide me through this process, I created a mood board: essential for keeping track of the distribution of colours and their effect within the rooms.

On the first floor, reserved for guests, I drew inspiration from the colours of the artichoke: deep greens that can shift towards violet and pink. This is why the Liquidambar and Quercus rooms are painted in pink and green. Both colours are present in each suite, but with different emphases. For these two spaces, I chose two different Farrow & Ball whites: in Liquidambar, I used Elephant's Breath, which leans towards pink; while in Quercus, I used the warmer Shaded White, to balance the forest green of the wardrobe and the sage green of the bed. I wanted the small sitting room to be a space filled with colour and light, both abundant thanks to the large windows and the collection of objects and books dedicated to nature that the room contains. Here I chose Cromarty, a delicate greenish white.

For the attic, which is our private apartment, I opted for a shade with a poetic name: Borrowed Light. This pale blue is barely perceptible unless it's set against pure white. It pairs beautifully with the light blue of the panelling, the earthy green of the furniture and the brick fireplace. None of the wall colours are assertive: they are always understated, creating a sense of calm.

I recommend taking your time when choosing colours. Test them, live with them, observe how they change over the course of a day in both natural and artificial light. A mood board can be an invaluable tool for collecting images and inspirations to help visualize the whole. In short, let the colours feel familiar to you so that your home truly reflects those who live in it and conveys a sense of warmth and serenity to everyone who enters.

*Colours do more than define a space; they also shape our mood and the way we perceive our surroundings.*

The Hidden Life of TREES

# SUMMER

*Light, colour and endless days…*
*the season of long evenings with friends.*

With the arrival of summer and the approach of the holiday season, our days take on a more frenetic rhythm. Guests, who in the spring awaken us from the quiet of winter, now become more numerous, and so do the dinners we host in the meadow. It is a period of intense activity, not unlike the life of the bees in the woods, whose buzzing – together with the cicadas singing in the pines – provides a constant soundtrack to the long sunlit days.

*Dinners in the meadow, illuminated by lanterns, have a special, almost magical atmosphere.*

Alessandro spends hours tending the garden, pruning the hedges while keeping a watchful eye on the agapanthus, with their tall green stems crowned with large buds that seem to sway like snakes charmed by an invisible flute. The rows of lavender and helichrysum burst into bloom, filling the farmhouse with their fragrance. I love walking through the fields in the morning on my way to open the henhouse, and watching the bees at work. Thanks to all these flowers, their honey will carry a particular flavour that already inspires new recipes in my mind.

In the winter of 2020, during the covid lockdown, we decided to plant olive trees across the large meadows on the hills and the slope facing the house. It was a time of great uncertainty, yet we felt fortunate compared to the majority of people who were confined in city apartments. We decided to share our sense of gratitude by inviting others to adopt an olive tree: I posted a video explaining that, with a small contribution, each tree could be adopted and that we would take care of its roots so it might grow strong and healthy. 'A man should have a child, write a book and plant a tree,' says a Zen proverb. We were wholly unprepared for what followed. Within two weeks, 140 olive trees had been adopted, and the stories we received were beautiful, many of them deeply moving. I remember a pregnant woman who had just lost her mother: she chose two trees, one in memory of her mother and the other for the daughter soon to be born, wishing for them to remain close together. I like to think of this place as a collective of intentions, where our guests are surrounded by a goodness that transcends time and space, of which we are only the humble custodians.

Those summer dinners in the meadow, held by lantern light, are especially enchanting. At sunset, the mountains turn blue and silence falls over the valley, before it gradually fills with the song of crickets and the flicker of fireflies. Busy with preparations in the kitchen, I often steal a glance out of the side window, hoping to catch the look of wonder in the eyes of guests as they arrive. Descending the steps from the parking area, they glimpse the lavender and helichrysum in bloom: violet and yellow bands of flowers opening up into what feels like a natural amphitheatre of mountains, trees and clouds.

On cooler evenings, we set a table beneath the pergola, where the wisteria offers a little shelter. I have hung large bunches of dried flowers from the beams so that the space feels like a flowering grotto, and added a floor-standing lamp with a shade to give everything a warm glow. Large baskets of tartan blankets are placed in corners of the meadow for those who feel the chill as the night advances and the dew begins to settle. All around the house and garden, fado music and romantic ballads from Cesária Évora and Ornella Vanoni complete the enchantment.

I remember the evening that inspired this set-up. I was in England filming and stopped for a drink at a country inn with three members of the cast. It was late afternoon and the innkeepers set us up in a field at the back. One of the actors recognized the stones scattered across the freshly ploughed earth: they were flint. Talking and laughing, we ended up with blankets around our shoulders, gazing up at the starry sky. It was a shared moment of simple beauty. And now, when I step out on to the meadow at Le Gusciane, I realize that, in some way, I have recreated it. That image has remained with me, and each summer I can share it with our guests, reliving it together under the Tuscan stars.

HELICHRYSUM
43%

# SUMMER PANZANELLA

*A rustic salad made with stale bread, panzanella was once the typical lunch of farmhands, prepared in the fields during harvest season. Fresh, flavourful, yet hearty, it was the perfect meal for labourers working long hours under the sun. I remember my first panzanella vividly: I was nine years old, it was the last day of summer camp in Spianessa, near Pistoia, and our parents had come to pick us up. At lunchtime, the counsellors divided us into teams, and our group was assigned the task of making panzanella. I will never forget the laughter of my parents, their hands plunged into large basins as they squeezed the soaked bread.*

INGREDIENTS

*Serves 4*

- 350g (12oz) stale bread
- extra virgin olive oil
- 500g (1lb 2oz) cherry tomatoes
- 30g (½ cup loosely packed) basil leaves
- 1 buffalo mozzarella ball, about 100g (3½oz), or 1 burrata cheese, about 150g (5½oz) (both optional)
- 2 peaches, about 300g (10½oz) total weight
- 1 red onion
- 2 tablespoons red wine vinegar
- salt and freshly ground black pepper

Preheat the oven to 180°C (350°F), Gas Mark 4.

Cut the bread into cubes. Arrange in a baking tray, brush with olive oil and season with salt. Bake for 10 minutes, or until golden, then leave to cool.

Meanwhile, halve the cherry tomatoes, place them in a bowl with the basil, dress with a little olive oil and season with salt and pepper. Cut the mozzarella or burrata, if using, into large chunks, then peel and dice the peaches and add both to the tomatoes. Slice the onion and place it in a bowl, mixing it with 4 tablespoons of olive oil and the red wine vinegar using a fork so the dressing absorbs the onion's flavour.

About 15 minutes before serving, put the toasted bread cubes in a salad bowl with the vinaigrette and the tomato mixture, then toss everything together, adjusting the seasoning with salt and pepper, depending on the sweetness of the peaches. Place the mozzarella or burrata, if using, on top.

It's important not to refrigerate panzanella, otherwise the bread will lose its crispness.

# AUBERGINE À LA GITANE

*One of my favourite memories from my years in the Big Apple was brunch at Café Gitane on Mott Street in Nolita. Gitane was a true pioneer in a neighbourhood that, in the early 1990s, was still filled with fabric warehouses and industrial supply shops. The little café – where at the time you could even smoke – was a real gem. I can still picture the steamed-up windows glowing with warm light when viewed from the outside, and smell the fragrance of Moroccan spices drifting through the air...*

*In the photo, I used different pestos for the aubergine slices (see Trio of Pestos, page 33), so you could try that, if you like.*

INGREDIENTS

*Serves 4*

- 2 aubergines (eggplant), about 500g (1lb 2oz) total weight
- 60–80ml (¼–⅓ cup) extra virgin olive oil, plus extra for brushing and the tapenade
- chilli flakes
- 1 garlic clove
- 1 tablespoon pine nuts
- 50g (½ cup) grated pecorino cheese
- 50g (½ cup) grated Parmesan cheese
- 40g (2 cups loosely packed) basil leaves
- 100g (½ cup) black olives
- palmful of thyme leaves
- 1 block of feta cheese, about 150g (5½oz)
- 4 slices of bread
- salt

Preheat the oven to 180°C (350°F), Gas Mark 4 and line a baking tray with baking paper. Slice the aubergines into 2cm (¾-inch) rounds, place on the prepared tray, then brush with olive oil, sprinkle with salt and a pinch of chilli flakes and roast for 20 minutes.

Prepare the pesto, ideally using a mortar and pestle, though a food processor will work just as well. Crush the garlic clove (remove the germ first) and pine nuts together. Add a pinch of salt, then the pecorino and Parmesan, followed by the basil leaves and measured olive oil. Work into a smooth paste.

Transfer the pesto to a bowl and rinse the mortar, ready to prepare the tapenade. Remove the pits from the olives and crush the flesh with the thyme, a pinch of chilli flakes and a drizzle of olive oil. The olives are likely already salty, so no extra seasoning is needed.

Crumble the feta by hand and stir it into the pesto. Spread this mixture over the roasted aubergines, which should now be soft in the centre. Return to the oven to brown, while you toast the bread. Serve the aubergines with the toasted bread and the olive tapenade on the side.

# AUBERGINE TARTARE

*Every time I visit London, my friends in the city introduce me to new neighbourhoods. One of my most recent discoveries was Coal Drops Yard, the redeveloped area behind King's Cross station, where old coal depots have been transformed into a vibrant shopping district full of boutiques and restaurants. Among them, Coal Office truly surprised me; their version of this dish simply won me over. After going back several times, I think I've managed to capture the essence of it in this recipe.*

INGREDIENTS
*Serves 4*

- ½ garlic clove
- 3 aubergines (eggplant)
- 3 tablespoons extra virgin olive oil, plus extra for brushing
- 40g (2 cups loosely packed) celery leaves
- 100g (⅔ cup) shelled unsalted pistachios
- 100g (½ cup) Taggiasca olives
- 200g (7oz) cherry tomatoes
- 4–5 mint leaves, thinly sliced
- 2 tablespoons apple cider vinegar
- juice of 1 lime
- salt and freshly ground black pepper

Preheat the oven to 180°C (350°F), Gas Mark 4 and line a baking tray with baking paper. Peel and thinly slice the garlic, using a small knife or mandoline.

Cut the aubergines into 2cm (¾-inch) slices. Score the flesh twice on one side of each slice and slip a sliver of garlic into each cut. Brush the slices with olive oil and arrange them in the prepared tray. Roast for about 20 minutes, making sure not to overcook them: the flesh should soften without drying out.

Meanwhile, purée the celery leaves with the measured olive oil, salt and pepper using a hand blender. Crush the pistachios in a mortar and stir into the purée along with the olives. Chop the cherry tomatoes into very small pieces and let them rest in their juices, mixed with the sliced mint leaves.

When the aubergines are ready (you'll see the garlic peeking out from the roasted flesh), remove them from the oven and allow to cool. Separate the skins from the flesh with a knife or spoon; discard the skins and the softened garlic slices. Cut the flesh into 1cm (½-inch) cubes.

Combine all the components in a bowl, adding vinegar, lime juice and salt to taste. The secret of this dish lies in the balance between the acidity of the vinegar and lime and the freshness of the mint, so, as you season, keep tasting until you find the perfect harmony.

STAUB

# VANESSA'S RATATOUILLE

*Vanessa is a strong and capable woman, someone you don't mess with, and I have a deep affection for her. Over the years, our lives have drifted apart, but we've never truly lost each other: we are connected, and that will never change. Our friendship has remained solid since we were in our twenties, when we would cry together on the couch over youthful heartbreaks. As the Romans would say, 'Vanessa è bella, bulla e balla bene': she's beautiful, fierce and fearless, and her French roots shine in the kitchen. From her many recipes, I've chosen her ratatouille, because when Vanessa speaks French, she silences us all with her flawless accent. And really, who wouldn't want a dish with such an enchanting accent?*

INGREDIENTS
*Serves 4*

- extra virgin olive oil
- 1 large onion, finely chopped
- 1 yellow pepper, deseeded and diced
- 1 red pepper, deseeded and diced
- 3 whole garlic cloves
- 600ml (2½ cups) tomato passata, homemade or store-bought
- 20g (1 cup loosely packed) basil leaves, chopped
- 1 carrot, peeled but left whole
- 4 thyme sprigs
- 2 large aubergines (eggplant), about 600g (1lb 5oz) total weight, thinly sliced
- 3 courgettes (zucchini), about 400g (14oz) total weight, preferably the light green Roman variety, thinly sliced
- 200g (7oz) tomatoes, halved or quartered
- 1 chilli, halved or quartered, to taste
- salt

In a deep saucepan or cast-iron dish, warm about 70ml (5 tablespoons) of olive oil and gently sauté the onion without browning.

Add the diced peppers and cook for a few minutes. Add the whole garlic cloves and cook for another 3 minutes.

Stir in the passata, basil and a good pinch of salt. Add the whole carrot and thyme sprigs. Simmer gently for about 15 minutes. Remove the garlic, carrot and thyme sprigs.

Preheat the oven to 180°C (350°F), Gas Mark 4.

Pour the sauce into a baking dish, spreading it evenly across the bottom. Arrange the aubergines, courgettes and tomatoes on top, alternating them from the outer edge towards the centre of the dish in a neat, visually pleasing pattern.

Season the vegetables with olive oil, salt and chilli. Cover the dish with foil and bake for 40 minutes. Remove the foil and continue baking for another 20 minutes, or until the vegetables are tender.

Let the ratatouille rest for a few minutes before serving. Finish with a drizzle of olive oil and a pinch of salt, if needed.

# SAVOURY CHEESECAKE

*Some people have been so important in shaping who I am that calling them mere 'friends' would be reductive. Chiara is one of those: a friend, a sister and above all a guide, she has always challenged me to look deeper, to ask more of myself, to see beyond. Chiara is always searching for answers, and during the weeks I spent as her guest in Los Angeles, she made me read books, join group meditations and talk. We would talk for hours, late into the night, often over a plate of pasta or some improvised dish such as this cheesecake, which we made every time we managed to find a mozzarella in California that was worthy of the name.*

**INGREDIENTS**
*Serves 4*

*For the cheesecake*

- 200g (7oz) stale bread
- extra virgin olive oil
- 2 thyme sprigs
- 1 mozzarella ball, ideally fior di latte, about 100g (3½oz)
- 100g (½ cup) cottage cheese, drained
- 1 burrata cheese, about 150g (5½oz)
- 400g (14oz) mixed cherry tomatoes
- pinch of dried oregano
- salt

*For the pesto*

- 1 tablespoon pine nuts
- 50g (½ cup) grated pecorino or Parmesan cheese
- 30g (1½ cups loosely packed) basil leaves
- 60ml (¼ cup) extra virgin olive oil

Preheat the oven to 180°C (350°F), Gas Mark 4 and line a baking tray with baking paper. Cut the bread into cubes. In a bowl, toss them with olive oil, thyme and salt, then bake for 10 minutes, or until golden.

Prepare the pesto. If using a mortar and pestle, there's a precise sequence; if using a food processor, you can add everything at once. In a mortar, crush the pine nuts, pressing them against the sides for a fine texture. Add salt, then the pecorino or Parmesan, followed by the basil leaves and olive oil.

Tear the mozzarella by hand and mix it in a bowl with the drained cottage cheese, then add the burrata and combine until smooth.

Dice the cherry tomatoes and season with olive oil, salt and oregano.

When ready to serve, assemble the cheesecake directly on the plate using a pastry ring: use the toasted croutons to form the base, then add the creamy cheese mixture, pressing gently with a spoon to create a flat surface, then top with the tomatoes. Finish with a spoonful of pesto on top.

# GREEN CRÊPES, OJAI STYLE

*Years ago, in Ojai, California, my friend Rachel took me to a little restaurant with a unique atmosphere, hidden away next to a farm, for an unforgettable afternoon snack. Rachel knew every corner of Ojai, and, between laughter and long conversations, she introduced me to spinach crêpes – perfect for a light lunch. Their simplicity, with the rich, earthy flavour of spinach, immediately won me over, making me appreciate the meeting of nature and cuisine even more. This recipe is a culinary gift I owe to Rachel.*

INGREDIENTS
*Serves 4*

*For the crêpes*

- 3 eggs
- 250g (2 cups) plain flour
- 500ml (2 cups) whole milk
- 200g (7oz) fresh spinach
- 2 tablespoons extra virgin olive oil, plus extra for cooking
- salt

*For the filling*

- 1 head of radicchio, about 250g (9oz)
- 100g (3½oz) rocket, plus extra to serve
- 1 ripe avocado, about 150g (5½oz)
- 2 green tomatoes, about 200g (7oz) total weight
- 150g (¾ cup) cottage cheese
- 100g (½ cup) soft goats' cheese

*For the vinaigrette*

- juice of 1 lime
- a few drops of piri piri sauce (optional)
- 3 tablespoons extra virgin olive oil
- freshly ground black pepper

To prepare the crêpes, beat the eggs with a pinch of salt in a large bowl. Add the flour and stir well. Gradually whisk in the milk to avoid lumps. Add the spinach and olive oil, then blitz everything together with a hand blender until smooth. Let the batter rest for about 30 minutes.

Warm a nonstick pan and lightly oil it. Pour in a ladleful of batter to form a crêpe about 5mm (¼ inch) thick. Cook for 2–3 minutes on each side until golden. Set aside but keep warm. Repeat until all the batter is used.

For the filling, separate the radicchio leaves and wash them along with the rocket. Slice the radicchio into thin strips. Peel and slice the avocado and dice the green tomatoes. In a bowl, combine the cottage cheese and goats' cheese.

In another bowl, whisk together all the ingredients for the vinaigrette, seasoning generously with salt and pepper.

To assemble, spread the radicchio, rocket, avocado and green tomatoes evenly over each crêpe. Add the cheese mixture, drizzle with the vinaigrette and fold or roll the crêpes, whichever you prefer.

Serve scattered with a few rocket leaves and a sprinkle of freshly ground black pepper.

# POTATO TORTELLI WITH VEGETARIAN RAGÙ

*This was my father's favourite dish. My grandmother Ottavia (the eighth of twelve siblings) used to make hundreds of tortelli for her grandchildren's afternoon gatherings in the Casentino. My father, who had moved to Prato when he was young, loved to tell us about how he would gorge himself on these tortelli. He bragged about eating more than fifty all by himself, and I still can't imagine how, since they were quite large. I have vivid memories of my grandmother rolling out the pasta on the board that my grandfather Renato had fixed to the table, while he stood by, commenting on her every move.*

INGREDIENTS
*Serves 4*

*For the dough*

- 170g (1¼ cups) plain flour, or pasta and pizza flour, plus extra for dusting
- 30g (¼ cup) semolina, plus extra for dusting
- 2 eggs
- about 100ml (½ cup) whole milk
- salt

*For the filling*

- 180g (6oz) potatoes
- 15g (¾ cup) parsley leaves
- 1 garlic clove
- extra virgin olive oil (optional)
- 1 tablespoon tomato purée (optional)
- 3 tablespoons grated Parmesan cheese, plus extra to serve
- nutmeg
- freshly ground black pepper
- 1 quantity Vegetarian Ragù for Marco (see page 27)

Make the pasta dough in a large bowl by mixing the flour and semolina with the eggs and a pinch of salt. Keep the milk to hand, adding splashes to soften the dough once the eggs have been fully absorbed into the flour. Knead until you obtain a firm ball of dough, then wrap it in a damp tea towel and refrigerate for 30 minutes.

Meanwhile, peel the potatoes and boil them in a saucepan of water until tender. Finely chop the parsley along with a small piece of the garlic clove. Use just a little garlic if adding raw, or you can sauté the whole finely chopped garlic clove with the parsley in olive oil, then add a spoonful of tomato purée, which gives the filling more colour. Check the potatoes with a fork; once done, drain and mash them with a potato masher. Mix with the garlic and parsley, Parmesan and grated nutmeg to taste (I like to add plenty). Season generously with salt and pepper.

After the pasta dough has rested, roll it out with a rolling pin until it's about 1mm (1/32 inch) thick, or use a pasta machine to reach the same thickness. Shape the filling into balls about 2cm (¾ inch) in diameter and place them about 5cm (2 inches) apart on one half of the sheet of dough. Fold the dough over, press down around the filling balls to remove the air and cut into ravioli with a pastry wheel. Place them on a tray dusted with semolina.

Cook the tortelli in a large saucepan of salted water. Meanwhile, warm the vegetarian ragù in a large pan or wok, adding a little cooking water to loosen it. Remove the tortelli with a slotted spoon and transfer them to the ragù pan, stirring gently into the sauce. Toss with some Parmesan, using a spatula and being careful not to break them.

Serve with freshly ground black pepper and plenty more Parmesan.

# CELERIAC MEDALLIONS

*This recipe was given to me by Filippo, a renowned restaurateur in Pietrasanta. Credit also goes to Andrea Papa, his talented chef. Filippo, outgoing and charismatic, has turned his restaurant – Filippo Pietrasanta – into a landmark for minimal design and innovative cuisine. One evening, Andrea served us this delicious dish. I spent months trying to recreate it without success, until finally, struck (or exhausted) by my determination, Andrea gave in and shared the recipe with me. It's a dish that requires a certain level of skill, but it never fails to impress at the table.*

INGREDIENTS
*Serves 4*

- 2 heads of celeriac, about 1kg (2lb 4oz) total weight
- dash of lemon juice
- 3–4 tablespoons extra virgin olive oil
- 1 large carrot, finely chopped
- 2 celery sticks, finely chopped
- 1 large onion, finely chopped
- 120ml (½ cup) white wine
- 1–2 tablespoons soy sauce
- aromatic herbal salt (80 per cent salt and 20 per cent sugar blended with rosemary and thyme leaves)

Thoroughly scrub the celeriac, then peel off and discard the skin. Soak the celeriac in a bowl of cold water with a little lemon juice for a few minutes, to remove any remaining traces of soil and make it easier to slice. Using a knife, sculpt each celeriac into a cylindrical shape, putting the offcuts to one side.

Once you have sculpted 2 cylinders, cut each one into 4 discs about 3cm (1¼ inches) thick. Using a vegetable peeler, go round and round the narrow edge of each disk, peeling it into one long strip. Don't worry if a strip breaks – you can patch it together in the next step.

Lay the strips flat on your work surface, brush with olive oil and season with aromatic salt. Now rewind each strip to create a spiral medallion (see photo) and tie once or twice (as necessary) with kitchen string.

Finely chop the celeriac trimmings and place them in a pan with the carrot, celery and onion. Add the white wine and cook gently over a low heat for about 2 hours.

Preheat the oven to 200°C (400°F), Gas Mark 6. Transfer the spiral medallions to a baking sheet lined with baking paper and roast for about 40 minutes, turning halfway through so that the cooking juices coat both sides.

When the mixed vegetable base is ready, strain it and season with a splash of soy sauce (add carefully as it's strong). Return the liquid to a pan with any remaining celeriac cooking juices and finish the medallions in it, caramelizing well on both sides. Carefully remove the kitchen string from each medallion.

Spoon some of the sauce on to plates and drizzle a little over the medallions before serving.

# ROSALBA'S COLD RICE SALAD

*Every Italian family has its own version of rice salad. My mother, always quick in the kitchen, used to make hers with sausages and pickled vegetables. So for me, the version by Rosanna – Alessandro's mother, who is known as Rosalba by everyone in her hometown of Rocca Gloriosa – was a revelation. Rosalba's rice salad is wonderfully fresh, with ripe tomatoes, mozzarella, hard-boiled eggs and olives. The original version also includes chopped ham and canned tuna. That's how Rosalba serves it: with the meat and fish on the side, along with some mayonnaise, so that everyone can help themselves as they please. Ever since I discovered this delight, I can't get enough of it.*

INGREDIENTS
*Serves 4*

- 1kg (2lb 4oz) brown rice
- 4 ripe tomatoes on the vine, 300–350g (10–12oz) total weight
- about 100g (½ cup) pitted green olives
- 4 hard-boiled eggs
- 2 mozzarella balls, ideally fior di latte, 250–300g (9–10½oz) total weight
- extra virgin olive oil
- salt and freshly ground black pepper

*Optional toppings*

- 2–3 tablespoons mayonnaise
- caperberries
- canned tuna
- about 100g (3½oz) cooked ham, diced
- about 100g (3½oz) smoked scamorza cheese

Cook the rice according to the packet instructions, then drain, cooling it under cold running water. Meanwhile, wash and dice the tomatoes and place them in a large bowl.

Slice the olives and eggs into rounds and add them to the bowl. Dice the mozzarella and add to the bowl with the olive oil to bring all the flavours together. Stir the rice into the mixture with a ladle until well combined. Season with salt and pepper to taste, then cover and refrigerate for 1 hour so the flavours meld.

Serve with mayonnaise on the side, and, if you like, top the salad with caperberries, tuna, ham and smoked scamorza.

# SCARPACCIA

*This was one of the first local specialities I discovered when I arrived in Camaiore. On Good Friday, the town celebrates the Passion of Christ with a procession known as Gesù Morto: the entire city is lit up with candles placed on the façades of the houses, a breathtaking sight. Invited to Isabella's home that evening, I was introduced to this delicious savoury tart. Everyone who tastes it is always surprised to find that there are no eggs in the recipe; instead, it relies on the liquid released by courgettes as they are salted.*

INGREDIENTS
*Serves 4*

- 750g (1lb 10oz) courgettes (zucchini)
- 1 teaspoon salt
- 1 onion
- 4 tablespoons extra virgin olive oil, plus extra for the dish
- 130 g (1 cup) strong white bread flour, or plain flour
- 40g (⅓ cup) fine polenta (not quick-cook)
- leaves from 1 rosemary sprig, finely chopped
- freshly ground black pepper

Wash the courgettes and slice them into rounds. If they have blossoms attached, clean and tear them into pieces. You can also use a mandoline for speed and even slices.

Salt the courgettes evenly with the teaspoon of salt and place them in a colander for about 1 hour, setting a plate and a weight on top to help press out their liquid and putting a bowl underneath the colander to collect the precious courgette water that will slowly be released. Meanwhile, finely chop the onion.

Preheat the oven to 200°C (400°F), Gas Mark 6.

After 1 hour, mix together the oil, the collected courgette water, the flour and polenta to form a smooth batter.

In a large bowl, combine the courgettes with the batter until well incorporated. Spread the mixture evenly in a greased nonstick baking dish, making sure the thickness is uniform. The dish I tend to use for this is round and 28cm (11 inches) in diameter; choose an equivalent-sized dish in which the batter will lie 0.5–1cm (¼–½ inch) deep.

Bake for 30 minutes, until a golden crust forms on top. Leave to rest for 5 minutes, then serve with a sprinkle of pepper and rosemary.

# SAVOURY TARTE TATIN

*This recipe was born of Alessandro's love for dishes with French names: the sound of the word 'ratatouille' has always amused him, but tarte Tatin is the one he repeats endlessly, enchanted by both the words and the theatrical moment when the tart is flipped upside down. I find tarte Tatin wonderfully flavourful and like to make variations of it, such as this. Caramelized onions add a distinctly French touch, but you can also finish it with crumbled ricotta salata and basil leaves.*

**INGREDIENTS**
*Serves 4*

*For the caramelized onions*

- 2 onions, 300–350 g (10–12oz) total weight
- 2 tablespoons extra virgin olive oil
- 2 tablespoons balsamic vinegar
- 1 tablespoon brown sugar

*For the tart*

- 2 tablespoons extra virgin olive oil, plus extra for the dish and to serve
- 1 tablespoon balsamic vinegar, plus extra for the dish
- 3 vine tomatoes, 350–400g (12–14oz) total weight
- 100g (3½oz) feta cheese, plus extra to serve
- 4–6 basil or thyme leaves, plus extra to serve
- 1 teaspoon clear honey
- 2 tablespoons pine nuts
- 1 sheet of ready-rolled puff pastry, about 230g (8oz)
- 1 egg yolk
- 1 burrata cheese, about 150g (5½oz), optional
- salt and freshly ground black pepper

Thinly slice the onions and place them in a frying pan with the oil, balsamic vinegar and brown sugar. Cover and cook over a low heat for about 20 minutes, stirring occasionally, until soft and caramelized.

Preheat the oven to 180°C (350°F), Gas Mark 4. Line a round baking dish with baking paper, drizzle with olive oil and balsamic vinegar and season with salt and pepper. Slice the tomatoes and arrange them on the paper, starting from the centre and working outwards in a spiral. Crumble over the feta, add the caramelized onions, season with more salt and pepper and scatter with the basil or thyme.

In a small bowl, mix together the honey, 1 tablespoon balsamic vinegar and 2 tablespoons olive oil and drizzle this mixture over the tomatoes. Scatter the pine nuts on top.

Cover with the puff pastry, tucking the edges snugly around the filling, then brush the surface with beaten egg yolk. Bake for about 30 minutes, until the pastry is golden.

Let the tart cool slightly. Place a serving plate upside down over the baking dish and, with a swift motion, invert the tart on to the plate. Remove the baking paper.

Top with crumbled feta and, if you like, place the burrata in the centre and cut into it to release its creamy core. Finish with a drizzle of olive oil and a scattering of basil or thyme leaves.

# PANCAKES WITH YOGURT AND HONEY

*The year I graduated from high school, my friend Marco and I set off on a memorable trip to San Diego, a month-long study break that gave us our first taste of the United States. One morning in Las Vegas, after a night wandering the Strip, we found ourselves back at our shabby motel, where we were served pancakes. They came in a towering stack, fluffy and perhaps a little too sweet, but unforgettable. I love to recreate them at the farmhouse, serving them with tangy Greek yogurt and our own honey.*

INGREDIENTS
*Serves 4*

- 200g (1½ cups) plain flour
- 65g (⅓ cup) caster (superfine) sugar
- 1 teaspoon baking powder
- 1 egg
- 250ml (1 cup) whole milk

*To serve (per person)*

- 50–100g (¼–½ cup) Greek yogurt
- 1 teaspoon honey
- fresh raspberries and blueberries, about 50g (½ cup)
- mint leaves (optional)
- about 1 tablespoon chopped walnuts (optional)
- about 1 teaspoon chocolate shavings (optional)

In a large bowl, combine the flour and sugar. Add the baking powder and whisk well. In a separate bowl, beat the egg, then add the milk and stir until smooth. Pour the wet mixture into the dry ingredients and stir until you have a lump-free batter.

Warm a nonstick frying pan over a medium heat. Pour in a ladleful of batter to form a small round. You should be able to cook about 4 at a time, depending on the size of your pan. Cook for 2–3 minutes per side, until golden and cooked through. Repeat with the remaining batter. You can keep the pancakes warm in a low oven while you finish cooking the rest of the batch.

Stack the pancakes on plates. Add a generous spoonful of Greek yogurt on the side. With the back of a spoon, create a small well in the yogurt and drizzle honey into it. Scatter with fresh raspberries and blueberries. For an extra touch, sprinkle with mint leaves, chopped walnuts or chocolate shavings.

# ALE'S TIRAMISU

*Even though I've never had much of a sweet tooth, tiramisu holds a special place in my heart. Being born in August meant I always celebrated my birthday away from schoolfriends, at the seaside. At Bagno Angelo Ponente, Pina, the owner of the beach club, would always have a big homemade tiramisu waiting for us at the bar when we came out of the water. That simple treat, with a candle stuck in its centre, always made me feel special. More than thirty years later, tiramisu has become Alessandro's signature dessert. He makes it for our guests at Le Gusciane, and every time I taste it, I'm taken straight back to those happy afternoons at the bar with Pina.*

INGREDIENTS
*Serves 4*

- 4 eggs
- 750g (3 cups) mascarpone cheese
- 50g (¼ cup) caster (superfine) sugar
- 300ml (1¼ cups) strong coffee, preferably Moka-style, cooled
- 36–42 Pavesini biscuits or ladyfingers
- grated dark chocolate, for sprinkling

Separate the eggs, placing the whites in the bowl of a stand mixer if you're using one. Beat the egg whites until stiff peaks form. Gently fold in the mascarpone with a spatula, working from the bottom up. Add the sugar and finally the yolks, blending everything into a thick, golden cream.

Pour some of the cooled coffee into a shallow bowl. Briefly dip one-third of the Pavesini or ladyfingers in the coffee, one at a time, taking care not to soak them too much, and arrange them in a baking dish. Cover the first layer of biscuits with one-third of the mascarpone cream. Sprinkle with grated chocolate before moving on to the next layer of biscuits and cream. Continue until you have 3 layers.

Finish with a generous grating of dark chocolate on top. Cover the dish and refrigerate for at least 2 hours before serving.

# SUMMER PEACH CARPACCIO

*Whenever my friend Eleonora invites me to her beach club in Forte dei Marmi, we find ourselves chatting under the cool shade of the canniccio. She is an extraordinary woman, gifted with both deep sensitivity and sparkling humour. Every summer, she spends her holidays in Versilia with her family at one of the area's historic beach resorts. There they serve a simple fruit salad of perfectly ripe peaches, brightened with mint leaves. That combination of flavours inspired this recipe: a dish that captures the very essence of summer in each bite, offering a light and refreshing finale to a meal.*

INGREDIENTS
*Serves 4*

- 4–5 peaches
- 2–3 mint leaves, plus a few shredded mint leaves to serve
- 1 tablespoon acacia honey
- bee pollen

Wash the peaches and slice them thinly with a mandoline, creating petal-like slices. Cut along the sides of each peach, leaving the centre with the pulp still attached to the pit. I later collect that pulp, slice it and set it aside to use in the centre of the plate.

Wash the mint leaves and tear them into a small bowl with a spoonful of water. Doing this by hand helps prevent oxidation from the knife blade, as well as leaving your fingers lightly scented with mint as you plate the dish.

Arrange the peach slices in concentric circles on each plate, placing the smaller pieces of pulp underneath, in the centre.

Stir the honey into the mint water so it thins slightly, then drizzle it gently all over the peach slices, including the pulp in the centre.

Finish with a dusting of bee pollen and shredded mint leaves and serve immediately.

## THE GARDEN: *A Sanctuary for the Soul*

Our farmhouse garden is Alessandro's great passion, to which he dedicates every spare moment. The hours of the day pass amid the chorus of cicadas and the sound of his rake on the gravel, which he tends with almost obsessive care. Sometimes I hear him talking and I lean out of the window, thinking someone has arrived, only to find him chatting with the wisteria (which, if left unchecked, would take over and wrap the house entirely in its embrace). Plants grow, and Alessandro prunes them, waters them, feeds them and coddles them with his thoughts spoken out loud.

Alessandro was fundamental in shaping our decision to move here. We live on the edge of a forest, and he takes care of everything outside the house with the same devotion and attention, from the chickens to the hydrangeas. Nothing makes him more proud than his garden. When he finds a guest who shares his passion, they can spend hours walking the grounds together, exchanging advice and ideas.

One of these encounters was with Warrie Price, a remarkable woman who, in her youth, spent time at the White House as the best friend of Gerald Ford's daughter. She is the founder and president of the Battery Conservancy in New York and has dedicated years to shaping the city's green planning. Warrie reached out to us a few years ago after hearing about Le Gusciane, and it was she who explained to Alessandro the importance of seeing the garden as something alive, in constant evolution.

For me, a garden must have a soul. I like the idea of plants 'looking at each other', creating a visual and natural connection between themselves. Often, we draw inspiration from what grows spontaneously in the surrounding countryside. In his book *The Hidden Life of Trees*, Peter Wohlleben describes how the plant kingdom communicates through roots and pollen, even across distance. I love flowering borders, and I have a fondness for perennials such as cistus, teucrium, loropetalum and ornamental sages. They not only add beauty with their blossoms, but are also hardy and enduring plants. Alessandro enjoys adding aromatic herbs, such as rosemary, marjoram and thyme, which are as pleasing to the eye as they are useful to the cook. It is important to place them thoughtfully, finding the right spot so they can help each other to ward off pests. Lavender and helichrysum, for example, are the perfect pairing to keep unwanted insects away.

It is wonderful to create specific areas in the garden, even away from the main house, offering corners of beauty and tranquillity. Some ideas came from my friend Duncan Cargill, who left his career as a PR executive to dedicate himself entirely to gardens. One suggestion was to create a bocce court, inspired by a small place on the marina in Sausalito, California. Benches, too, should be placed in well-considered spots that open on to a captivating view, though a single armchair beneath the shade of a tree can also create a small haven of peace and serenity. Just as I like to create wells of light with lamps inside the house (see page 117), in the garden I like to imagine spaces that offer moments of reflection and quiet.

The garden is a refuge, a place of meeting and communion with nature, but it is also a living work of art, continually evolving, shaped by the passion and dedication of the one who tends it.

*The garden is a refuge, a place to gather and to meet, a space where we reconnect with nature.*

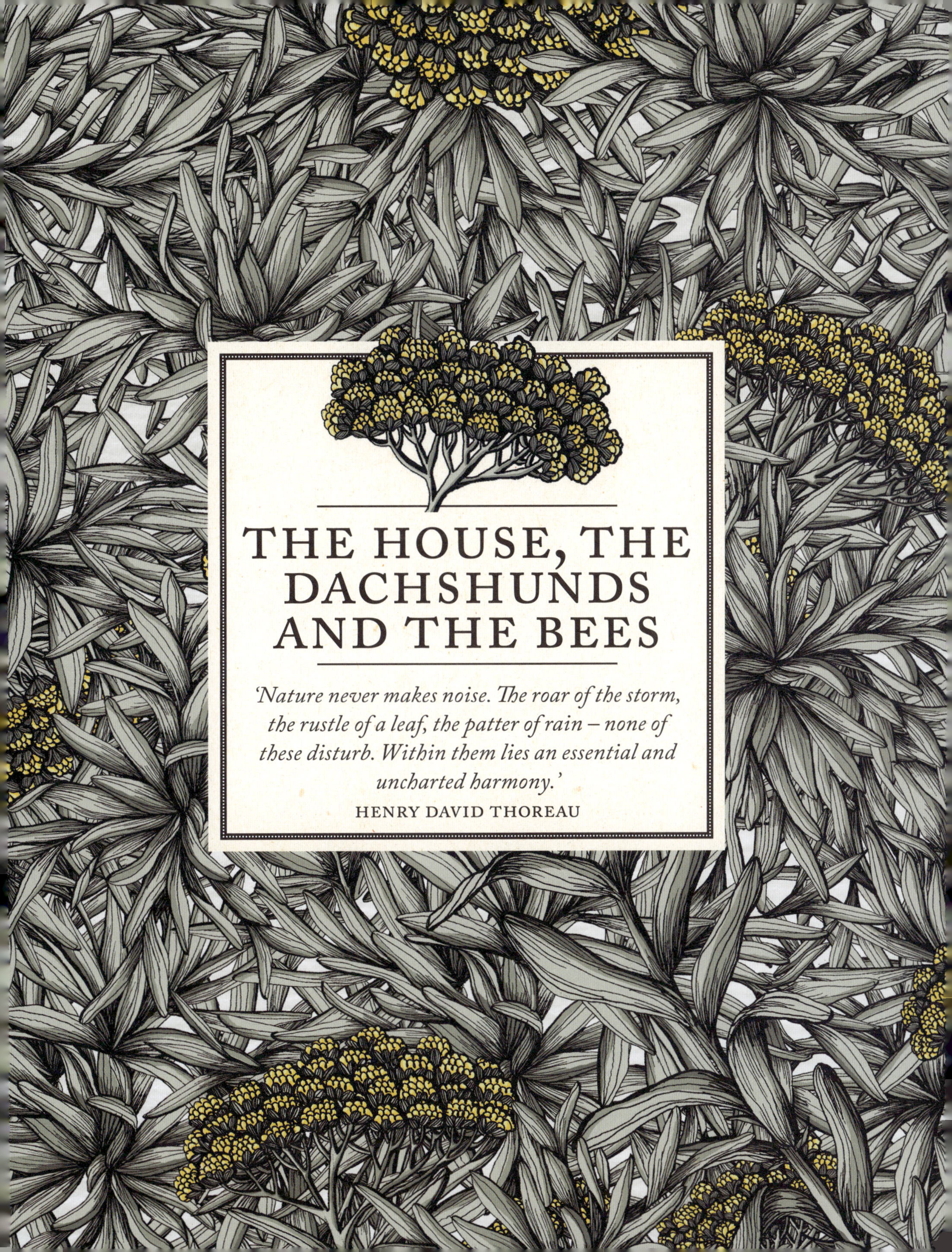

# THE HOUSE, THE DACHSHUNDS AND THE BEES

*'Nature never makes noise. The roar of the storm, the rustle of a leaf, the patter of rain – none of these disturb. Within them lies an essential and uncharted harmony.'*

HENRY DAVID THOREAU

# THE HOUSE

When I first laid eyes on Le Gusciane, I knew I had found a truly special place. The farmhouse seemed as though it had been painted by a 19th–century romantic, immersed in a sea of olive trees and cypresses, with a wide chestnut and oak forest at its rear and a sweeping view of the Camaiore valley, framed by mountains.

Here began my adventure in creating what I like to call the 'Lovely Tuscan Lifestyle'. It is a way of living that embraces the warmth of the Nordic concept of hygge and the rustic beauty of English cottagecore, but with an Italian soul.

This land, once under the custodianship of the Giannini family, has witnessed generations grow, prosper and depart. From their hilltop on Montemagno, the Gianninis were the guardians of Pontemazzori, and the small metato (chestnut-drying house) built in 1860, which has become Le Gusciane, remains a testament to another era. It is easy to picture both weathered and youthful hands at work here, gathering chestnuts, peeling and drying them with care and transforming them into chestnut flour, the true grain of the forest.

When we took over the property, the farmhouse revealed architectural secrets of its own. In 1906, an expansion had reshaped the building to accommodate a farmhand in service to the lords of the main villa. The western wing, with its new façade, absorbed the old metato and created a mosaic of eras and styles. It was fascinating to see how traces of the past intertwined with the present: the large 19th-century terracotta bricks, the chestnut beams replaced with pine in the following century, and the different proportions of the windows across the two wings of the house.

The very setting of Le Gusciane, with its sturdy stone walls, recalls the image of English country cottages, similar to those that dot the rolling hills of the Cotswolds. Letting my imagination wander, I began to weave a story.

I imagined that, in 1906, an eccentric English gentleman, profoundly shaped by the adventures of his youth – following in the footsteps of Byron and other explorers on a Grand Tour of Europe – decided to settle in sunlit Tuscany. In his later years, searching for a refuge near the sea, he was struck by the sight of this modest metato. Without hesitation he approached the Gianninis, the esteemed landowners of the valley, with a generous offer. Surprised yet pleased, they accepted, and the property changed hands. The dwelling was soon expanded, and the land surrounding it was reshaped in the spirit of English landscaping. Gardens designed to stir the emotions appeared, oases of peace, with benches placed in thoughtful corners where one could rest in the shade and contemplate the valley framed by mountains.

With the passing of time, Le Gusciane became a true refuge for this gentleman's descendants, and every corner of the house came to hold a fragment of their family history. An eccentric painting brought back from Paris by an aunt would find its place here, as would a cousin's baroque armchair or a grandmother's Bloomsbury-style lamp. The home gradually filled with objects and memories, forming a patchwork of stories and affections.

As a director, I drew inspiration from this imagined history, much as a set designer would for a film. I used its narrative to guide my choices in furnishing the interiors, giving Le Gusciane an ambience that is warm, singular and rich with meaning. It is the same atmosphere with which we love to welcome our guests, inviting them to make our house their own, even if only for a while.

Le Gusciane

# THE DACHSHUNDS

Our dachshunds, whom we affectionately call 'the Zen Masters', deserve a section of their own. I have Alessandro to thank for wanting to adopt them, for sensing the need for them before I did.

Gastone, Camillo, Furio and Borlotto are the most enthusiastic welcoming committee one could imagine. Their joy is contagious, their affection irresistible, and I am endlessly amused watching them win over even the most dog-sceptic of visitors. Perseverance is their secret weapon. No guest ever leaves the farmhouse without pausing to wish them a proper farewell. They are a small but tightly knit pack: they eat together, play together and sleep curled up together, yet each has a distinct personality that could fill pages and pages… though I will limit myself to one paragraph each.

## Gastone

Gastone's coat is chocolate brown, his short hair coarser along his back, while the gentle arch of his nose and his almond-shaped eyes give him an aristocratic air that matches his general distrust of the elements. If it rains, Gastone stays in. If the gravel outside is too cold, he tiptoes across it. He is a little gentleman, elegant in movement, but often a touch clumsy. Gastone almost never barks; in fact, it happens so rarely that, when it does, it always takes us by surprise. What makes him truly endearing is his awkwardness. If I am standing in the entrance hall talking with someone, he will climb a few steps of the staircase just to reach my cheek and try to kiss me. Or, if I call him in my deepest voice – 'Gastooone' – and he is in the garden, he stiffens, arches his back and rolls over, waiting for kisses and cuddles.

## CAMILLO

Camillo, Gastone's brother, is the very image of the perfect dachshund. He plays fetch, he never disobeys and, unlike his siblings – often caught up in the bustle of the pack – he stays focused on us. To tell the truth, I am his chosen one, which moves me deeply. Camillo is never more than a step away from me. If I head to the toolshed, sit under the pergola to write, or start cooking in the kitchen, he settles close by and watches me with quiet devotion. And if he finds me sitting in an armchair, he will not rest until I take him in my arms. When I finally do, he showers me with kisses, insistent and unstoppable, until he curls up in my lap. Only then can I admire the beauty of his silver harlequin coat, the black heart-shaped marking on his back, and scratch behind his ears to hear his contented little rumble.

## FURIO

Furio arrived about a year after Gastone and Camillo. Jet black, with ears so long he nearly trips over them, he was both comical and independent from the start. Tireless and fearless, Furio is our little panther, with a coat as glossy as silk. Joining an already-bonded clan was no small feat, but the others welcomed him kindly. He is the dog who most asserts his individuality, always the first to dash outside in the morning, rain or shine; the first to chase after any creature we encounter in the woods. He eats with the appetite of a wolf, wasting no time on ceremony, and like the others he is never shy about showing affection. Often, when I sit down to write in the morning, Furio comes to me, wanting to climb on my lap, often ending up tucked inside my sweatshirt like a kangaroo Joey. This lasts until our youngest dog, Borlotto, inevitably joins us.

## BORLOTTO

Borlotto, unlike the others, was born here, under this very roof, and that alone makes him feel different. He came into the world on 7 May 2020, and it was my daughter Bianca who chose his name. When her dachshund Mafalda became pregnant after mating with our Gastone, she had already decided that one of the puppies would be called Borlotto. With his marbled coat and striking blue eyes, he was a heart-stealer from the very beginning. Like many youngest siblings, he has a talent for getting into trouble, but he wins us over every time with his irresistible charm. He does not climb into your lap, he leaps into your arms, and when you hold him, he melts completely, pressing himself into the hollow of your neck just as he did when he was no bigger than an aubergine.

*These four creatures are a blessing. To care for them is to receive a gift in return. Their companionship enriches us, reminding us of the importance of simplicity and unconditional love. They warm the heart and make every moment feel special.*

## THE BEES

One of the most ambitious projects we embarked upon at the farmhouse was our apiary. Before committing to it, we visited others and immersed ourselves in their world, determined to be prepared. We knew the scale of the investment of time and money involved, but also the crucial role these creatures play in the ecosystem. Foraging bees pollinate within a radius of three or four kilometres (2–2½ miles), sustaining life far beyond their hive.

But for us, the project held a deeper meaning. In the months following the pandemic, I had spent much time reflecting on mental health, reading widely on the subject. Along the way, I discovered the astonishing universe of bees, a world that captivated me. Their society is a model of balance and purpose. Each bee is born with a task, or a sequence of tasks that shift over the course of its life. They travel miles alone, find the coordinates of a blooming field, then return to the hive to share it with their clan. They are individuals, yet they move as if part of a single organism, the hive itself.

Together with Alessandro, I wanted to share this lesson at Le Gusciane. The word 'bee' and the verb 'to be' seemed to invite a meditation. I selected a series of qualities, each paired with one of our hives, as a way to spark reflection and bring awareness to the beauty of positive states of being.

From this grew what I call 'The Wisdom of Bees', life lessons that I also recorded in a series of meditative podcasts.

## THE WISDOM OF BEES

1 *Bee Adventurous*
To be adventurous like the bees means approaching life's challenges with courage and curiosity. Every exploration reveals new parts of ourselves and of the world, unfolding another piece of our essence. The truest adventure is the journey inward, begun with a single step of trust.

2 *Bee Brave*
Bees show their bravery in defending the hive and facing danger head on. In our lives too, courage is not the absence of fear, but the will to act in spite of it, meeting each trial with strength and resolve.

3 *Bee Caring*
Nurse bees embody tenderness and care. To follow their example is to nurture our relationships, our dreams and ourselves. Love begins with self-compassion and from there radiates outward, enriching our spirit and the bonds we share.

4 *Bee Compassionate*
Compassion in the hive teaches us empathy. When we place ourselves in another's shoes, we deepen our understanding and open the way to harmony in our connections.

5 *Bee Confident*
Forager bees, sure of their mission, remind us to trust our instincts. Confidence grows from self-awareness and inner listening, guiding us towards choices that are genuine and fulfilling.

6 *Bee Creative*
The artistry of bees in crafting their hive inspires us to connect with our own creativity. Whether in art, food or the way we shape our lives, creativity allows us to transform the everyday into beauty and meaning.

7 *Bee Cheerful*
Like bees that begin each day with energy, we too can cultivate joy. Even in difficult moments, simple gestures can rekindle lightness, filling both our world and those around us with positive energy.

8 *Bee Clever*
Bees use collective intelligence to solve problems. We, too, can draw on learning, experience and imagination to create, innovate and grow.

9 *Bee Enthusiastic*
Bees bring enthusiasm to their work. The word 'enthusiasm' literally means 'being with God'. When we operate from that place we become co-creators of our own reality.

10 *Bee Enlightened*
The wisdom of bees lies in their connection to the whole. To be enlightened is to live with awareness, recognizing that we are part of something greater, and finding gratitude in that belonging.

11 *Bee Everything*
Throughout their lives, bees take on many roles. They show us how to adapt, grow and embrace each stage of life with authenticity and wholeness.

12 *Bee Fervent*

As bees keep their hive warm through the winter, we too must nurture our dreams with perseverance and devotion. Passion and resolve sustain us through challenges and guide us toward our goals.

13 *Bee Fierce*

The tenacity of bees in protecting their hive inspires us to defend our values. To be fierce is to stand strong in the face of adversity, looking forward with courage and hope.

14 *Bee Funny*

Even in their ordered world, bees find moments of play. So too should we embrace humour, laughter and the ability not to take ourselves too seriously amid life's complexities.

15 *Bee Generous*

Bees share their honey with the hive. Their generosity reminds us that giving freely enriches both giver and receiver, creating bonds of gratitude and joy.

16 *Bee Gentle*

Gentleness in the hive shows us how kindness softens the world. To be gentle is to move through life with openness, creating safety and trust in our relationships.

17 *Bee Genuine*

Bees live true to their purpose. Likewise, to be genuine is to be honest with ourselves and with others, expressing thoughts and feelings without pretence.

18 *Bee Gifted*

Each bee has a unique gift that sustains the hive. By recognizing and honouring our own talents, we contribute to the whole and fulfil our potential.

19 *Bee Giving*

The selflessness of bees inspires us to give without expectation. Generosity of heart connects us deeply with others and enriches our shared lives.

20 *Bee Grateful*

In their tireless work, bees embody gratitude. To be grateful is to honour the beauty in what we have and what we experience, facing challenges with a spirit of appreciation.

21 *Bee Happy*

As bees find joy in their labour, we too can cultivate happiness in the everyday. Presence, gratitude and delight in small things open us to a full and satisfying life.

22 *Bee Honest*

Bees operate with integrity, a reminder that honesty is the foundation of trust. To be honest is to live with clarity and transparency in all we do.

23 *Bee Humble*

The humility of bees, working tirelessly for the hive, teaches us to respect limits and appreciate the contributions of others. Humility opens the door to growth.

24 *Bee Independent*
Bees display independence in their tasks, showing us the power of self-reliance. To be independent is to move forward with faith in our own capacity and direction.

25 *Bee Intuitive*
Guided by instinct, bees find their way to nectar. Likewise, we can listen to our inner voice, trusting intuition as a compass towards authenticity.

26 *Bee Kind*
The author Charlie Mackesy says that nothing beats kindness; it sits gently with everything and enhances all.

27 *Bee Patient*
Step by step, bees build their hive. Patience teaches us that progress takes time, and that each small effort is part of a larger unfolding.

28 *Bee Passionate*
Bees live with devotion and energy. To be passionate is to pour our hearts into what we love, filling our lives with warmth and vibrancy.

29 *Bee Soulful*
In their deep connection with the world, bees remind us to live with soul. To be soulful is to embrace the richness of feeling and the depth of human experience.

30 *Bee Strong*
The strength of bees lies in their unity. To be strong is to draw upon our inner reserves and rise through challenges with resilience.

31 *Bee Tender*
Bees nurture each other with tenderness. To be tender – especially with ourselves – allows us time to understand and forgive ourselves.

32 *Bee Thoughtful*
The thoughtfulness of bees in caring for their hive reminds us to act with consideration. Thoughtfulness means listening, observing and offering compassion.

33 *Bee True*
Bees live in harmony with their purpose. To be true is to remain faithful to ourselves, to express our essence without masks and to live with authenticity.

# *acknowledgments*


Writing a book is a journey. Looking back, I realize that journey began long before I wrote the first page; it is the fruit of a lifetime of encounters, like shiny pebbles collected from the bed of a stream.

The first unexpected encounter was with Eloisa Bianco, whom I met one summer in Versilia when I was 14. More than 30 years later, it was she who introduced me to my publisher. So thank you, Eloisa, for introducing me to the EDT family, and to Luca Iaccarino, who was the first to believe in the project. Thanks to Isabella Maria, who gathered my ideas and set the framework for the work. To art director Paolo Racca, for interpreting my vision and enriching every page with his talent. To illustrator Andrea Tarella, for his creativity, sensitivity and generosity. To photographer Edoardo Colombo, who captured a year of life at our farmhouse in evocative, heartfelt images. To Benedetta Canale, for caring for each dish and making it special with her touch. To Elena Mazzetti and her team at Giardino delle Fate, for contributing to the table settings with their wonderful flowers and objects. To Stefano Kalogerakis, not only for the Staub pots, but also for being the first to read the book and offer precious advice. To Bitossi and Ginori, in the persons of Gian Maria Rebecchi and Rebecca Rizzello, for their contribution.

A special thank you to Tatiana, who first welcomed me to Camaiore with her enthusiasm, and shared with me the secrets of homemade pasta. To my friends Andrea, Vanessa, Clelia and many others who, over the years, have passed on their love for cooking, especially my restaurateur friends Filippo, Angiolo and Teo from Rome.

To my family; this book is filled with all of you, who first taught me the joy of sharing a meal with love. To the Franchini family, who welcomed me; to my friends Arcadio, Lisa, Lavinia, Francesca and Peter Spears, whose friendship and encouragement helped set this book on its path beyond Italy, and who are always by my side, cheering me on.

To our dogs, Gastone, Camillo, Furio, Borlotto and Mafalda: your sweet little faces add magic to my days. To all the guests of Le Gusciane, who inspire us every day to do better: thank you for your compliments and encouragement. Thanks to Anna Maria, our collaborator, who always restores order to my chaos, especially when I cook.

Thanks to Alessandro, my life and adventure companion: the dream of Le Gusciane grows every day, fuelled by your determination, imagination and creativity – none of it would be possible without you. Thank you for these eight years together and for always pushing me beyond my limits.

Finally, my heartfelt gratitude goes to the team at Aevitas Creative Management: David Kuhn and Nate Muscato in New York, and Gus Brown in the London office, as well as to Daniela Delfino, for guiding this project with care and expertise. And to my editor, Jeannie Stanley at Mitchell Beazley/Octopus, for her trust, insight and thoughtful guidance in bringing the English edition of this book to life.

*To my mother Emanuela,*
*who often burned the sauce.*

*To my daughter Bianca, who*
*I hope will one day turn to this*
*book to welcome her friends.*

## INDEX OF RECIPES

## MENU

### *Essentials*



### *Local Favourites*



### *Salads*



### *Mains*

*Desserts*

## ABOUT THE AUTHOR

After graduating from university in Prato – the city where he was born in 1974 – Luca Calvani moved to New York, where he worked for a textile company and began studying acting at the Actor's Studio. From there he embarked on an international career in film and television.

He made his big-screen debut in *Le fate ignoranti* by Ferzan Özpetek and went on to appear in major international productions, including *The International* directed by Tom Tykwer, *To Rome with Love* by Woody Allen, *The Man from U.N.C.L.E.* directed by Guy Ritchie, and the Bollywood hit *Shakuntala Devi* (2020). In 2023 he directed his first feature film, *Fosco and Fred*.

He has appeared in English-language television series such as *Sex and the City*, *As the World Turns*, *The Bold and the Beautiful* and *The Durrells in Corfu*. In Italy, he was the winner of the reality TV show *L'Isola dei Famosi* (Celebrity Island) in 2006; one of the three judges on *Cortesie per gli ospiti*, a competition show about home entertaining, in 2023; and took part in *Grande Fratello* (Big Brother) in 2024.

Alongside his work on screen, he pursues his passion for hospitality and gastronomy. In the Tuscan hills, together with his husband Alessandro Franchini, he runs the farmhouse *Le Gusciane*, where he oversees the kitchen and culinary experiences. The recipes born there are collected in this, his first book, *A Tuscan* Table, originally published in Italy under the title *Cavoli & Merende*, which has also become a cooking show for the Food Network, bringing his world of seasonal Tuscan vegetarian cuisine and countryside living to an international audience.